IT SERVICE MANAGE
A POC

D0373856

service management art
Guidance for process improvement

(+1-403) 219 4195
www.servicemanagementart.com

About the ITSM Library

The publications in the ITSM Library cover best practice in IT management and are published on behalf of itSMF International.

The IT Service Management Forum (itSMF) is the association for practitioners and organizations who practice ITSM. itSMF's goal is to promote innovation and IT management. Suppliers and customers are equally represented within the itSMF. The Forum's main focus is exchange of peer knowledge and experience. Our authors are global experts.

The following publications are, or soon will be, available.

Introduction, Foundations and Practitioners books
- Foundations of IT Service Management based on ITIL® (V2, Arabic, Chinese, German, English, French, Italian, Japanese, Korean, Dutch, Brazilian Portuguese, and Russian; Danish and Spanish)
- Foundations of IT Service Management based on ITIL® (V3, English, Dutch)
- IT Service Management - An Introduction (V2, being replaced by V3, only a few languages left)
- IT Service Management - An Introduction (V3, English, Dutch)
- IT Services Procurement based on ISPL - An Introduction (Dutch)
- Project Management based on PRINCE2™ 2005 Edition (Dutch, English, German)

Release & Control for IT Service Management, based on ITIL® - A Practitioner Guide (English)

IT Service Management - best practices
- IT Service Management - best practices, part 1 (Dutch)
- IT Service Management - best practices, part 2 (Dutch)
- IT Service Management - best practices, part 3 (Dutch)
- IT Service Management - best practices, part 4 (Dutch)

Topics & Management instruments
- Metrics for IT Service Management (English)
- Six Sigma for IT Management (English)
- The RfP for IT Outsourcing - A Management Guide (Dutch)
- Service Agreements - A Management Guide (English)
- Frameworks for IT Management (English, German, Japanese)
- IT Governance based on COBIT® - A Management Guide (English, German)

Pocket guides
- IT Service Management - A summary based on ITIL® (V2, Dutch)
- IT Service Management based on ITIL V3 - A Pocket Guide (V3, English, Dutch)
- ISO/IEC 20000 - A Pocket Guide (English, German, Japanese, Italian, Spanish, formerly BS 15000 - A Pocket Guide)
- IT Services Procurement based on ISPL - A Pocket Guide (English)
- IT Service CMM - A Pocket Guide (English)
- Six Sigma for IT Management - A Pocket Guide (English)
- Frameworks for IT Management - A Pocket Guide (English, Dutch)

Miscellaneous
- IT Service Management from Hell!! (V2, English)
- IT Service Management from Hell. Based on Not-ITIL (V3, English)

For any further enquiries about ITSM Library, please visit www.itsmfbooks.com, http://en.itsmportal.net/en/books/itsm_library or www.vanharen.net.

IT Service Management Based on ITIL® V3

A POCKET GUIDE

*it*SMF International
The IT Service Management Forum

A publication of itSMF International

Colophon

Title:	IT Service Management Based on ITIL V3 - A Pocket Guide
Editors (Inform-IT):	Jan van Bon (chief editor)
	Arjen de Jong (co-author)
	Axel Kolthof (co-author)
	Mike Pieper (co-author)
	Ruby Tjassing (co-author)
	Annelies van der Veen (co-author)
	Tieneke Verheijen (co-author)
Publisher:	Van Haren Publishing, Zaltbommel, www.vanharen.net
Design & layout:	CO2 Premedia bv, Amersfoort - NL
ISBN:	978 90 8753 102 7
Edition:	First edition, first impression, November 2007

Foreword

The long-awaited update of ITIL®, launched in June 2007, presents a rigorously updated source of best practices on IT service management. For most of the existing practitioners, trainers, consultants and other users of ITIL V2 documentation, there are significant changes as ITIL V3 follows quite a different approach. The updated version introduces the Service Lifecycle as the main structure for its guidance, whereas V2 is mainly based on processes and functions.

This concise summary offers a very practical and valuable introduction to the content of the five new ITIL V3 core books. It explains the structure and way of thinking of the new Service Lifecycle. In addition, by presenting the information about processes and functions in a separate section, it also provides support for all the existing users of V2 that are looking for a bridge to the new edition. This second section shows all the elements that were present in the Foundation-scope of ITIL V2, as well as all new processes, functions and main activities of V3.

The resulting pocket guide provides the reader with a quick reference of the basic concepts of ITIL V3. Readers can use the itSMF publication "Foundations of IT Service Management based on ITIL V3" or the ITIL core volumes (Service Strategy, Service Design, Service Transition, Service Operation and Continual Service Improvement) for more detailed understanding and guidance.

This pocket guide was produced in the same way as other publications of the ITSM Library: a broad team of expert editors, expert authors and expert reviewers contributed to a comprehensive text, and a great deal of effort was spent on the development and review of the manuscript.

I'm convinced that this new pocket guide will provide an excellent reference tool for all those practitioners, students and others who want a concise summary of the key ITIL V3 concepts.

Jan van Bon
Managing Editor ITSM Library

Acknowledgements

Following the official publication of ITIL V3, this pocket guide was developed as a concise summary of the ITIL V3 core books, by the authors of the itSMF publication "Foundations of IT Service Management - Based on ITIL V3". For reasons of continuity the Review Team of the Foundation title was the base for the pocket guide Review Team. Additionally, all members of IPESC, itSMF International's Publication Committee, were invited to participate in the review. Thirteen itSMF chapters actively participated in the review, with effectively seventeen reviewers that provided comments after reviewing the text.

The integrated Review Team was composed of the following:
- Rob van der Burg, Microsoft, Netherlands
- Judith Cremers, Getronics PinkRoccade Educational Services, Netherlands
- Dani Danyluk, Burntsand, itSMF Canada
- John Deland, Sierra Systems, itSMF Canada
- Robert Falkowitz, Concentric Circle Consulting, itSMF Switzerland
- Karen Ferris, itSMF Australia
- Peter van Gijn, LogicaCMG, Netherlands
- Jan Heunks, ICT Partners, Netherlands
- Kevin Holland, NHS, UK
- Ton van der Hoogen, Tot Z Diensten BV, Netherlands
- Matiss Horodishtiano, Amdocs, itSMF Israel
- Wim Hoving, BHVB, Netherlands
- Brian Johnson, CA, USA
- Steve Mann, SM2 Ltd, itSMF Belgium
- Reiko Morita, Ability InterBusiness Solutions, Inc., Japan
- Ingrid Ouwerkerk, Getronics PinkRoccade Educational Services, Netherlands

- Ton Sleutjes, Capgemini Academy, Netherlands
- Maxime Sottini, iCONS – Innovative Consulting S.r.l., itSMF Italy

These reviewers spent their valuable hours on a detailed review of the text, answering the core question "Is the content a correct reflection of the core content of ITIL V3, given the limited size of a pocket guide?". Providing several hundreds of valuable improvement issues, they contributed significantly to the quality of this pocket guide, and we thank them for that.

The review process was managed by Mike Pieper, managing editor at Inform-IT. He managed the development of this pocket guide, making sure that the procedures were followed carefully, and that all issues were followed up to the satisfaction of all reviewers. The editorial support was provided by another five expert editors from Inform-IT's Editors Team:
- Arjen de Jong
- Axel Kolthof
- Ruby Tjassing
- Annelies van der Veen
- Tieneke Verheijen

Due to the expert services of the Review Team and the professional support by the Editors Team, the resulting pocket guide is a great new asset for the itSMF, providing an excellent entry into the core ITIL V3 books. We are very satisfied with the result, which will be of great value for people wanting to get a first high-level grasp of what ITIL V3 is really all about.

Jan van Bon,
Chief Editor "IT Service Management Based on ITIL V3 - A pocket Guide"
Managing Editor ITSM Library

Contents

1   Introduction

This pocket guide provides the reader with a quick reference of the basic concepts of ITIL version 3 (ITIL V3). Part 1 describes the Service Lifecycle as documented in ITIL V3 and part 2 describes the associated processes and functions.

Readers can use the publication "Foundations of IT Service Management based on ITIL V3" or the ITIL core volumes (Service Strategy, Service Design, Service Transition, Service Operation and Continual Service Improvement) for more detailed understanding and guidance.

1.1   What is ITIL?

The Information Technology Infrastructure Library™ (ITIL) offers a systematic approach to the delivery of quality IT services. ITIL was developed in the 1980s and 1990s by CCTA (Central Computer and Telecommunications Agency, now the Office of Government Commerce, OGC), under contract to the UK Government. Since then, ITIL has provided not only a best practice based framework, but also the approach and philosophy shared by the people who work with it in practice. ITIL has now been updated two times, the first time in 2000-2002 (V2), and the second time in 2007 (V3).

Several organizations are involved in the maintenance of the best practice documentation in ITIL:
- *OGC (Office of Government Commerce)* - Owner of ITIL, promoter of best practices in numerous areas including IT Service Management.
- *itSMF (IT Service Management Forum)* - A global, independent, internationally recognized not-for-profit organization dedicated to support the development of IT Service Management, e.g. through publications in the ITSM Library series. It consists of a growing number

of national chapters (40+), with itSMF International as the controlling body.

- *APM Group* - In 2006, OGC contracted the management of ITIL rights, the certification of ITIL exams and accreditation of training organizations to the APM Group (APMG), a commercial organization. APMG defines the certification and accreditation schemes for the ITIL exams, and publishes the associated certification system.
- *Exam bodies* - To support the world-wide delivery of the ITIL exams, APMG has accredited (at the time of publishing this pocket guide) a number of exam bodies: EXIN, BCS/ISEB, and Loyalist Certification Services (LCS).

1.2   ITIL exams

In 2007 the APM Group launched a new certification scheme for ITIL, based on ITIL V3. ITIL V2 will be maintained for a transition period, continuing up until at least the year 2008.

ITIL V2 has qualifications on three levels:
- *Foundation Certificate* in IT Service Management
- *Practitioner's Certificate* in IT Service Management
- *Manager's Certificate* in IT Service Management

The ITIL V2 exams proved to be a great success. Up to 2000, some 60,000 certificates had been issued, in the following years the numbers rocketed, and by 2006 had broken the 500,000 mark.

For ITIL V3 a completely new system of qualifications has been set up. There are four qualification levels:
- *Foundation level* - This level is aimed at basic knowledge of, and insight into, the core principles and processes of ITIL V3. This qualification is positioned at the same level as the ITIL version 2 Foundation exam.

- *Intermediate level* (based on two work streams, one based on the Service Lifecycle, and one based on practitioner capabilities).
- *Advanced level* - This level was still under development when this pocket guide was being written.

For each element in the scheme a number of credits can be obtained, that can be used to obtain the ITIL V3 Diploma. Credits are also awarded for the certificates from the ITIL version 2 scheme. Various 'bridge exams' are offered in order to upgrade version 2 certificates to the version 3 qualifications.

Further information on the actual status of this system can be found at the APMG website: www.apmgroup.co.uk.

1.3 Structure of this pocket guide

The body of this pocket guide is set up in two Parts: Part 1 deals with the ITIL V3 Service Lifecycle, Part 2 deals with the individual functions and processes that are described in ITIL V3.

Part 1 starts with Chapter 2, introducing the Service Lifecycle, in the context of IT Service Management general principles.

In Chapters 3 to 7, each of the phases in the Service Lifecycle is discussed in detail, following a standardized structure: Service Strategy, Service Design, Service Transition, Service Operation and Continual Service Improvement.

Part 2 starts with Chapter 8, introducing the functions and processes that are referred to in each of the lifecycle phases. This chapter provides general information on principles of processes, teams, roles, functions, positions, tools, and other elements of interest. It also shows how the 27 processes and functions are clustered in the 5 ITIL core books.

In Chapters 9 to 13, the processes and functions are described in more detail. For each process and function, the following information is provided:

- Introduction
- Basic concepts
- Activities
- Inputs/Outputs

1.4   How to use this pocket guide

Readers who are primarily interested in getting a quick understanding of the Service Lifecycle can focus on Part 1 of the pocket guide, and pick whatever they need on functions and processes from Part 2.

Readers who are primarily interested in an overview of the functions and processes in ITIL can focus on the functions and processes of their interest, described in Part 2.

This way, the pocket guide provides support to a variety of approaches to IT Service Management based on ITIL.

PART 1
THE ITIL SERVICE LIFECYCLE

2 Introduction to the Service Lifecycle

2.1 Definition of Service Management

ITIL is presented as a *good practice*. Good practice is an approach or method that has proven itself in practice. Good practices can be a solid backing for organizations that want to improve their IT services.

The ITIL Service Lifecycle is based on ITIL's core concept of "service management" and the related concepts "service" and "value". These core terms in service management are explained as follows:

- *Service management* - A set of specialized organizational capabilities for providing value to customers in the form of services.
- *Service* - A means of delivering value to customers by facilitating outcomes the customers want to achieve without the ownership of specific costs or risks. Outcomes are possible from the performance of tasks and they are limited by a number of constraints. Services enhance performance and reduce the pressure of constraints. This increases the chances of the desired outcomes being realized.
- *Value* - Value is the core of the service concept. From the customer's perspective, value consists of two core components: utility and warranty. Utility is what the customer receives, and warranty is how it is provided. The concepts "utility" and "warranty" are described in the Section "Service Strategy".

2.2 Overview of the Service Lifecycle

ITIL V3 approaches service management from the lifecycle aspect of a service. The Service Lifecycle is an organizational model that provides insight into:

- The way service management is structured.
- The way the various lifecycle components are linked to each other.

- The impact that changes in one component will have on other components and on the entire lifecycle system.

Thus, ITIL V3 focuses on the Service Lifecycle, and the way service management components are linked. Processes and functions are also discussed in the lifecycle phases.

The Service Lifecycle consists of five phases. Each volume of the new ITIL describes one of these phases. The related processes are described in detail in the book in which they find their key application.
The five phases (domains of the core books) are:
1. Service Strategy
2. Service Design
3. Service Transition
4. Service Operation
5. Continual Service Improvement

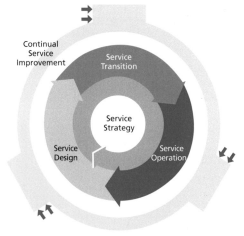

Figure 2.1 The Service Lifecycle

Service Strategy is the axis of the Service Lifecycle (Figure 2.1) that drives all other phases; it is the phase of policymaking and setting objectives. The Service Design, Service Transition and Service Operation phases are guided by this strategy, their continual theme is adjustment and change. The Continual Service Improvement phase stands for learning and improving, and embraces all other lifecycle phases. This phase initiates improvement programs and projects, and prioritizes them based on the strategic objectives of the organization.

3 Lifecycle Phase: Service Strategy

3.1 Introduction

In this section, the axis (principle line of development, movement, direction, reference point) of the lifecycle is introduced. As the axis of the lifecycle, Service Strategy delivers guidance with designing, developing and implementing service management as a strategic asset. Service Strategy is critical in the context of all processes along the ITIL Service Lifecycle.

The mission of the Service Strategy phase is to develop the capacity to achieve and maintain a strategic advantage.

The development and application of Service Strategy requires constant revision, just as in all other components of the cycle.

3.2 Basic concepts

To formulate the strategy, Mintzberg's four Ps are a good starting point (Mintzberg, 1994):
- *Perspective* - Have a clear vision and focus.
- *Position* - Take a clearly defined stance.
- *Plan* - Form a precise notion of how the organization should develop itself.
- *Pattern* - Maintain consistency in decisions and actions.

Value creation is a combination of the effects of utility and warranty. Both are necessary for the creation of value for the customer. For customers, the positive effect is the "utility" of a service; the insurance of this positive effect is the "warranty":
- *Utility - fitness for purpose*. Functionality offered by a product or service to meet a particular need. Utility is often summarized as "what it does".

- *Warranty - fitness for use.* A promise or guarantee that a product or service will meet its agreed requirements. The availability, capacity, continuity and information security necessary to meet the customers' requirements.

The *value networks* are defined as follows: "A value network is a web of relationships that generate both tangible and intangible value through complex and dynamic exchanges between two or more organizations."

Resources and capabilities are the *service assets* of a service provider. Organizations use them to create value in the form of goods and services.
- *Resources* - Resources include IT Infrastructure, people, money or anything else that might help to deliver an IT service. Resources are considered to be the assets of an organization.
- *Capabilities* - Capabilities develop over the years. Service providers must develop distinctive capabilities in order to maintain services that are difficult to duplicate by the competition. Service providers must also invest substantially in education and training if they are to continue to develop their strategic assets and maintain their competitive advantage.

Service providers are organizations that supply services to one or more internal or external customers. Three different types of service providers are distinguished:
- *Type I: Internal service provider* - An internal service provider that is embedded within a Business Unit. There may be several type I service providers within an organization.
- *Type II: Shared Services Unit* - An internal service provider that provides shared IT services to more than one Business Unit.
- *Type III: External service provider* - A service provider that provides IT services to external customers.

The *Service Portfolio* represents the opportunities and readiness of a service provider to serve the customers and the market space. The Service Portfolio can be divided into three subsets of services:
- *Service Catalogue* - The services that are available to customers.
- *Service Pipeline* - The services that are either under consideration or in development.
- *Retired Services* - Services that are phased out or withdrawn.

3.3   Processes and other activities

This section briefly explains the processes and activities of Service Strategy. More information about each of these processes can be found in Chapter 9 of this pocket guide.

The Service Strategy processes:
- *Financial management* - An integral component of service management. It anticipates the essential management information in financial terms that is required for the guarantee of efficient and cost-effective service delivery.
- *Demand management* - An essential aspect of service management in which offer and demand are harmonized. The goal of demand management is to predict, as accurately as possible, the purchase of products and, where possible, to balance the demand with the resources.
- *Service Portfolio Management (SPM)* - Method to manage all service management investments in terms of business value. The objective of SPM is to achieve maximum value creation while at the same time managing the risks and costs.

The Service Strategy activities:
- *Defining the market* - Understand the relation between services and strategies, understand the customers, understand the opportunities, and classify and visualize the services.

- *The development of the offer* - Create a Service Portfolio that represents the opportunities and readiness of a service provider to serve the customers and the market.
- *The development of strategic assets* - Define the value network and improve capabilities and resources (service assets) to increase the service and performance potential.
- *Preparation for execution* - Strategic assessment, setting objectives, defining Critical Success Factors, prioritizing investments, et cetera.

3.4   Organization

There are five recognizable phases in organizational development within the spectrum of centralization and decentralization:

1. *Stage 1: Network* - An organization in stage 1 focuses on fast, informal and ad hoc provision of services. The organization is technologically oriented and is uncomfortable with formal structures.
2. *Stage 2: Directive* - In stage 2, the informal structure of stage 1 is transformed into an hierarchical structure with a strong management team. They assume the responsibility for leading the strategy and for guiding managers to embrace their functional responsibilities.
3. *Stage 3: Delegation* - In stage 3, efforts are made to enhance technical efficiency and provide space for innovation in order to reduce costs and improve services.
4. *Stage 4: Coordination* - In stage 4 the focus is directed towards the use of formal systems as a means of achieving better coordination.
5. *Stage 5: Collaboration* - During stage 5, the focus is on the improvement of cooperation with the business.

The goal of the Service Strategy is to improve the core competencies. Sometimes it is more efficient to outsource certain services. We call this the SoC principle (Separation of Concerns, SoC): that which results from the search for competitive differentiation through the redistribution of resources and capabilities.

The following generic forms of outsourcing can be delineated:

- *Internal outsourcing*:
  - Type 1 Internal - Provision and delivery of services by internal staff; this offers the most control, but is limited in scale.
  - Type 2 Shared services - Working with internal BUs; offers lower costs than Type 1 and more standardization, but is still limited in scale.
- *Traditional outsourcing*:
  - Complete outsourcing of a service - A single contract with one service provider; better in terms of scaling opportunities, but limited in best-in-class capabilities.
- *Multi-vendor outsourcing*:
  - *Prime* - A single contract with one service provider who works with multiple providers; improved capabilities and risks, but increased complexity.
  - *Consortium* - A selection of multiple service providers; the advantage is best-in-class with more oversight; the disadvantage is the risk of the necessity of working with the competition.
  - *Selective outsourcing* - A pool of service providers selected and managed through the service receiver; this is the most difficult structure to manage.
  - *Co-Sourcing* - A variation of selective outsourcing in which the service receiver combines a structure of internal or shared services with external providers; in this case, the service receiver is the service integrator.

3.5 Methods, techniques and tools

Services are socio-technical systems with service assets as the operational elements. The effectiveness of Service Strategy depends on a well-managed relationship between the social and technical sub-systems. It is essential to identify and manage these dependencies and influences.

Tools for the Service Strategy phase can be:

- *Simulation* - System Dynamics is a methodology for understanding and managing the complex problems of IT organizations.
- *Analytical modeling* - Six Sigma, PMBOK® and PRINCE2® offer well tested methods based on analytical models. They must be evaluated and adopted within the context of Service Strategy and service management.

Three techniques for quantifying the value of an investment are suggested:

- *Business case* - A way of identifying business objectives that are dependent on service management.
- *Pre-Program ROI* - Techniques used to quantitatively analyze investments before committing resources.
- *Post-Program ROI* - Techniques used to retroactively analyze investments.

3.6   Implementation and operation

Strategic goals are to be converted into plans with objectives and ultimate goals, based on the lifecycle. Plans translate the intentions of the strategy into actions, through Service Design, Service Transition, Service Operation, and Continual Service Improvement.

Service Strategy provides every phase of the lifecycle with input:

- *Strategy and design* - Service strategies are implemented through the delivery of the portfolio in a specific market area. Newly chartered services or services that require improvements in order to suit the demand are promoted to the Service Design phase. The design can be driven by service models, outcomes, constraints or pricing.
- *Strategy and transition* - To reduce the risk of failing, all strategic changes go through Service Transition. Service Transition processes analyze, evaluate and approve strategic initiatives. Service Strategy provides Service Transition with structures and constraints like the Service Portfolio, policies, architectures, and the contract portfolio.

- *Strategy and operations* - The final realization of strategy occurs in the production phase. The strategy must be in line with operational capabilities and constraints. Deployment patterns in Service Operation define operational strategies for customers. Service Operation is responsible for delivering the contract portfolio and should be able to deal with demand changes.
- *Strategy and CSI* - Due to constant changes, strategies are never static. Service strategies need to be developed, adopted and continually reviewed. Strategic imperatives influence quality perspectives processed in CSI. CSI processes deliver feedback for the strategy phase on for example: quality perspective, warranty factors, reliability, maintainability, redundancy.

Challenges and opportunities:
- *Complexity* - IT organizations are complex systems. This explains why some service organizations are not inclined to change. Organizations are not always in a position to anticipate the long-term consequences of decisions and actions. Without continual learning processes, today's decisions often end up as tomorrow's problems.
- *Coordination and control* - The people who make the decisions often have limited time, attention and capacity. Therefore they delegate the roles and responsibilities to teams and individuals. This makes coordination through cooperation and monitoring essential.
- *Preserving Value* - Customers are not only interested in the utility and warranty that they receive for the price they pay. They want to know the Total Cost of Utilization (TCU).
- *Effectiveness in measurement* - Measurements focus the organization on its strategic goals, follow the progression and provide the organization with feedback. Most IT organizations are good at monitoring data, but often they are not very good at providing insights into the effectiveness of the services that they offer. It is crucial to perform the right analyses and to modify them as the strategy changes.

The implementation of strategy leads to changes in the Service Portfolio. This involves management of related risks. Risk is defined as follows: "a risk is an uncertain outcome, or in other words, a positive opportunity or a negative threat." Risk analysis and risk management must be applied to the Service Pipeline and Service Catalogue in order to identify, curb and mitigate the risks within the lifecycle phases.

The following types of risks are recognized:
- contract risks
- design risks
- operational risks
- market risks

4 Lifecycle Phase: Service Design

4.1 Introduction

Service Design deals with the design and development of services and their related processes. The most important objective of Service Design is: the design of new or changed services for introduction into a production environment.

The Service Design phase in the lifecycle begins with the demand for new or changed requirements from the customer. Good preparation and an effective and efficient infusion of people, processes, products (services, technology and tools) and partners (suppliers, manufacturers and vendors) - ITIL's four Ps - is a must if the design plans and projects are to succeed.

4.2 Basic concepts

The design phase should cover five important aspects:

1. *The design of service solutions* - A structured design approach is necessary in order to produce a new service for the right costs, functionality, and quality, including all of the functional requirements, resources and capabilities needed and agreed. The process must be iterative and incremental in order to satisfy the customers' changing wishes and requirements. It is important to assemble a Service Design Package (SDP) with all aspects of the (new or changed) service and its requirements through each stage of its lifecycle.

2. *The design of the Service Portfolio* - The Service Portfolio is the most critical management system for supporting all of the processes. It describes the service delivery in terms of value for the customer and must include all of the service information and its status. In any event, the portfolio makes clear in which phase the service takes place; from defining the requirements until retiring of the service.

3. *The design of the architecture* - The activities include preparing the blueprints for the development and deployment of an IT infrastructure, the applications, the data and the environment (according to the needs of the business). This architecture design is defined as: "the development and maintenance of IT policies, strategies, architectures, designs, documents, plans and processes for deployment, implementation and improvement of appropriate IT services and solutions throughout the organization."

4. *The design of processes* - By defining what the activities in the lifecycle phases are and what the inputs and outputs are, it is possible to work more efficiently and effectively, and especially in a more customer-oriented way. By assessing the current quality of processes and the options for improvement, the organization can enhance its efficiency and effectiveness even further. The next step is to establish norms and standards. This way the organization can link the quality requirements with the outputs. This approach corresponds with Deming's *Plan-Do-Check-Act* Management Cycle.

5. *The design of measurement systems and metrics* - In order to lead and manage the development process of services effectively, regular assessments of service quality must be performed. The selected assessment system must be synchronized with the capacity and maturity of the processes that are assessed. There are four elements that can be investigated: *progress, fulfillment, effectiveness* and *efficiency of the process*.

The question which model should be used for the development of IT services largely depends on the **service delivery model** that is chosen. The delivery options are:

- *Insourcing* - Internal resources are used for the design, development, maintenance, execution, and/or support for the service.
- *Outsourcing* - Engaging an external organization for the design, development, maintenance, execution, and/or support of the service.

- *Co-sourcing* - A combination of insoucing and outsourcing in which various outsourcing organizations work cooperatively throughout the service lifecycle.
- *Multi-sourcing* - (or partnership) Multiple organizations make formal agreements with the focus on strategic partnerships (creating new market opportunities).
- *Business Process Outsourcing (BPO)* - An external organization provides and manages (part of) another organization's business processes in a low cost location.
- *Application service provision* - Computer-based services are offered to the customer over a network.
- *Knowledge Process Outsourcing (KPO)* - Knowledge of an process- or domain is offered.

Traditional **development approaches** are based on the principle that the requirements of the customer can be determined at the beginning of the service lifecycle and that the development costs can be kept under control by managing the changes. Rapid Application Development (RAD) approaches begin with the notion that change is inevitable and that discouraging change simply indicates passivity in regard to the market. The RAD-approach is an incremental and iterative development approach:

- *The incremental approach* - A service is designed bit by bit. Parts are developed separately and are delivered individual. Each piece support one of the business functions that the entire service needs. The big advantage in this approach is its shorter delivery time. The development of each part, however, requires that all phases of the lifecycle are traversal.
- *The iterative approach* - The development lifecycle is repeated several times. Techniques like prototyping are used in order to understand the customer-specific requirements better.

A combination of the two approaches is possible. An organization can begin by specifying the requirements for the entire service, followed by an incremental design and the development of the software. Many organizations however, choose standard software solutions to satisfy needs and demands instead of designing the service themselves.

4.3   Processes and other activities

This section briefly explains the processes and activities of the Service Design.

More information about each of these processes can be found in Chapter 10 of this pocket guide.

Service Design processes:
- *Service Catalogue Management (SCM)* - The goal of SCM is the development and maintenance of a Service Catalogue that includes all of the accurate details and the status of all operational services and those being prepared to run operationally, and the business processes they support.
- *Service Level Management (SLM)* - The goal of SLM is to ensure that the levels of IT service delivery are documented, agreed and achieved, for both existing services and future services in accordance with the agreed targets.
- *Capacity management* - The goal of capacity management is to ensure that the capacity corresponds to both the existing and future needs of the customer (recorded in a capacity plan).
- *Availability management* - The goal of the availability management process is to ensure that the availability level of both new and changed services corresponds with the levels as agreed with the customer. It must maintain in an Availability Management Information System (AMIS) which forms the basis the availability plan.
- *IT Service Continuity Management (ITSCM)* - The ultimate goal of ITSCM is to support business continuity (vital business functions, VBF)

by ensuring that the required IT facilities can be restored within the agreed time.

- *Information security management* - Information security management ensures that the information security policy satisfies the organization's overall security policy and the requirements originating from corporate governance.
- *Supplier management* - Supplier management draws attention to all of the suppliers and contracts in order to support the delivery of services to the customer.

Service Design technology-related activities:

- *Development of requirements* - Understanding and documenting the business and user's requirements (functional requirements, management- and operational requirements and usability requirements).
- *Data and information management* - Data is one of the most critical matters that must be kept under control in order to develop, deliver and support effective IT services.
- *Application management* - Applications, along with data and infrastructure, comprise the technical components of IT services.

4.4 Organization

Well performing organizations can quickly and accurately make the right decisions and execute them successfully. In order to achieve this, it is crucial that the roles (and responsibilities) are clearly defined. Amongst others, the roles include:

- Process owner
- Service design manager
- Service catalogue manager
- Service level manager
- Availability manager
- Security manager

4.5   Methods, techniques and tools

It is extremely important to ensure that the tools to be used support the processes and not the other way around. There are various tools and techniques that can be used for supporting the service and component designs. Not only do they make the hardware and software designs possible, but they also enable the development of environment designs, process designs and data designs. Tools help ensure that Service Design processes function effectively. They enhance efficiency and provide valuable management information on the identification of possible weak points.

4.6   Implementation and operation

In the following section the implementation considerations for Service Design are addressed.

* *Business Impact Analysis (BIA)* - BIA is a valuable source of information for establishing the customer's needs, and the impact and the risk of a service (on the business). The BIA is an essential element in the business continuity process and dictates the strategy to be followed for risk reduction and recovery after a catastrophe.

* *Implementation of Service Design* - Process, policy and architecture for the design of IT services, must be documented and used in order to design and implement appropriate IT services. In principle, they all should be implemented because all processes are related and often depend on each other. In this way you will get the best benefit. It is important do this in a structured way.

* *Prerequisites for Success (PFS)* - Prerequisites are often requirements from other processes. For example, before Service Level Management (SLM) can design the Service Level Agreement (SLA), a Business Service Catalogue and a Technical Service Catalogue are necessary.

KPIs for the Service Design process include:
- Accuracy of the SLAs, OLAs and UCs.
- Percentage of specifications of the requirements of Service Design produced within budget.
- Percentage of Service Design Packages (SDPs) produced on time.

Examples of challenges that are faced during implementation include:
- The need for synchronization of existing architecture, strategy and policy.
- The use of divers technologies and applications instead of single platforms.
- Unclear or changing customer requirements.

There are several risks during the Service Design phase, including:
- If the level of maturity in one of the processes is low, it is impossible to reach a high level of maturity in other processes.
- Business requirements are not clear for the IT personnel.
- Too little time is allotted for Service Design.

Figure 4.1 shows that the output from every phase becomes input to another phase in the lifecycle. Thus Service Strategy provides important input to Service Design, which in turn, provides input to the transition phase. The Service Portfolio provides information to every process in every phase of the lifecycle.

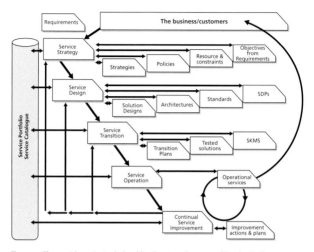

Figure 4.1 The most important relationships, inputs and outputs of Service Design

5 Lifecycle Phase: Service Transition

5.1 Introduction

Service Transition consists of the management and coordination of the processes, systems and functions required for the building, testing and deployment of new and changed services into operations. Service Transition establishes the services as specified in Service Design phase, based on the customer and stakeholder requirements.

A Service Transition is effective and efficient if the transition delivers what the business requested within the limitations in terms of money and other necessary resources, as determined in the Design phase.

An effective Service Transition ensures that the new or changed services are better aligned with the customer's business operation. For example: the capacity of the business to react quickly and adequately to changes in the market.

5.2 Basic concepts

The following *policies* are important for an effective Service Transition and apply to every organization. The approach does need to be adjusted to the conditions that are appropriate for each different organization:

- Define and implement guidelines and procedures for Service Transition.
- Implement all changes through Service Transition.
- Use common frameworks and standards.
- Re-use existing processes and systems.
- Coordinate Service Transition plans with the needs of the business.
- Create relations with stakeholders and maintain these.
- Set up effective controls on assets, responsibilities and activities.
- Deliver systems for knowledge transfer and decision support.

- Plan packages for releases and deployment.
- Anticipate and manage changes in plans.
- Manage the resources proactively.
- Continue to ensure the involvement of stakeholders in an early stage in the Service Lifecycle.
- Assure the quality of a new or changed service.
- Proactively improve service quality during a Service Transition.

5.3   Processes and other activities

A Service Transition generally comprises the following steps:

- planning and preparation
- building
- service testing and pilots
- planning and preparation of the deployment
- deployment, transition and retire
- review and closing of Service Transition

This section briefly explains the processes and activities of a Service Transition. More information about each of these processes can be found in Chapter 11 of this pocket guide.

Service Transition processes:

- *Transition planning and support* - Ensures the planning and coordination of resources in order to realize the specification of the Service Design.
- *Change management* - Ensures that changes are implemented in a controlled manner, i.e. that they are evaluated, prioritized, planned, tested, implemented, and documented.
- *Service Asset and Configuration Management (SACM)* - Manages the service assets and Configuration Items (CIs) in order to support the other service management processes.

- *Release and deployment management* - Aimed at the building, testing and deploying of the services specified in the Service Design, and ensures that the client can utilize the service effectively.
- *Service validation and testing* - Tests ensure that the new or changed services are "fit for purpose" and "fit for use".
- *Evaluation* - Generic process that is intended to verify whether the performance is acceptable; for example, whether it has the right price/ quality ratio, whether it is continued, whether it is in use, whether it is paid for, and so on.
- *Knowledge management* - Improves the quality of decision-making (for management) by ensuring that reliable and safe information is available during the Service Lifecycle.

Service Transition activities:
- *Communication* is central during every Service Transition.
- Significant change of a service also means a change of the organization. *Organizational change management* should address *the emotional change cycle* (shock, avoidance, external blame, self blame and acceptance), and *culture and attitudes*.
- *Stakeholder management* is a Crucial Success Factor in Service Transition. A stakeholder analysis can be made to find out what the requirements and interests of the stakeholders are, and what their final influence and power will be during the transition.

Although change management, SACM, knowledge management, and others, support all phases of the Service Lifecycle, the ITIL Service Transition book covers these. Release and deployment management, service validation and testing, and evaluation are included in the scope of Service Transition.

5.4   Organization

Service Transition is actively managed by a *Service Transition manager*. The Service Transition manager is responsible for the daily management and control of the Service Transition teams and their activities.

Generic roles are:
- Process owner - the process owner ensures that all process activities are carried out.
- Service owner - has the responsibility, toward the client, for the initiation, transition and maintenance of a service.

Other roles that can be distinguished within Service Transition include:
- Service asset manager
- Configuration manager
- Change manager
- Deployment manager
- Configuration analyst
- Configuration manager
- Configuration management system manager
- Risk-evaluation manager
- Service knowledge manager

Responsibility areas include:
- Test support
- Early Life Support
- Building and test environment management
- Change Advisory Board (CAB)
- Configuration management team

5.5   Methods, techniques and tools

Technology plays an important part in the support of Service Transition. It can be divided into two types:

- *IT Service Management systems* - Such as enterprise frameworks which offer integration opportunities linking with the CMS or other tools; system, network and application management tools; service dashboard and reporting tools.
- *Specific ITSM technology and tools* - Such as service knowledge management systems; collaboration tools; tools for measuring and reporting; test (management) tools; publishing tools; release and deployment technology.

5.6   Implementation and operation

The implementation of Service Transition in a "Greenfield" situation (from zero) is only likely when establishing a new service provider. Most service providers therefor focus on the improvement of the existing Service Transition (processes and services). For the improvement of Service Transition the following five aspects are important:

1. *Justification* - Show the benefits in business terms of effective service transition to all stakeholders.
2. *Design* - Factors to take into account when designing are standards and guidelines, relationships with other supporting services, project and program management, resources, all stakeholders, budget and means.
3. *Introduction* - Do not apply the improved or newly implemented Service Transition to current projects.
4. *Cultural aspects* - Even formalizing existing procedures will lead to cultural changes in an organization. Take this into consideration.
5. *Risks and advantages* - Do not make any decisions about the introduction or improvement of Service Transition without an insight into the risks and advantages to expect.

There is input/output of knowledge and experience from and to Service Transition. For example: Service Operation shares practical experiences with Service Transition as to how similar services behave in production. Also, experiences from Service Transition supply inputs for the assessment of the designs from Service Design. Like with processes in a process model, all phases in a lifecycle will have outputs that are inputs in another phase of that lifecycle.

For a successful Service Transition, several challenges need to be conquered, such as:
- Taking into account all stakeholders.
- Finding the balance between a stable operation environment and being able to respond to changing business requirements.
- Creating a culture in which one is responsive to cooperation and cultural changes.
- Ensuring that the quality of services corresponds to the quality of the business.
- A clear definition of the roles and responsibilities.

Potential risks of Service Transition are:
- de-motivation of staff
- unforeseen expenses
- excessive cost
- resistance to changes
- lack of knowledge sharing
- poor integration between processes
- lack of maturity and integration of systems and tools

6 Lifecycle Phase: Service Operation

6.1 Introduction

Service Operation involves coordinating and carrying out activities and processes required to provide and manage services for business users and customers within a specified agreed service level. Service Operation is also responsible for management of the technology required to provide and support the services.

Service Operation is an essential phase of the Service Lifecycle. If the day-to-day operation of processes is not properly conducted, controlled and managed, then well-designed and well-implemented processes will be of little value. In addition there will be no service improvements if day-to-day activities to monitor performance, assess metrics and gather data are not systematically conducted during Service Operation.

6.2 Basic concepts

Service Operation is responsible for the fulfillment of processes that optimize the service costs and quality in the Service Management Lifecycle. As part of the organization, Service Operation must help ensure that the customer (business) achieves their goals. Additionally, it is responsible for the effective functioning of components supporting the service.

Achieving balance in Service Operation:
- Handling a possible internal en external conflict between maintaining the current situations and reacting to changes in the business and technical environment. Service Operations must try to achieve a balance between conflicting priorities.
- Achieving an IT organization in which stability and response are in balance. On the one hand, Service Operation must ensure that the

IT infrastructure is stable and available. At the same time, Service Operation must recognize the business needs changes and must embrace change as a normal activity.

• Achieving an optimal balance between costs and quality. This addresses IT's challenge to continually improve the quality of services while at the same time reducing or at the very least maintaining costs.

• Achieving a proper balance in reactive and proactive behavior. A reactive organization does nothing until an external stimulus forces it to act. A proactive organization always looks for new opportunities to improve the current situation. Usually, proactive behavior is viewed positively, because it enables the organization to keep a competitive advantage in a changing environment. An over-proactive attitude can be very costly, and can result in distracted staff.

It is very important that the Service Operation staff are involved in Service Design and Service Transition, and, if necessary, in Service Strategy. This will improve the continuity between business requirements and technology design and operation by ensuring that operational aspects have been given thorough consideration.

Communication is essential. IT teams and departments, as well as users, internal customer and Service Operation teams, have to communicate effectively with each other. Good communication can prevent problems.

6.3   Processes and other activities

This section briefly explains the processes and activities of a Service Operation. There are some key Service Operation processes that must link together to provide an effective overall IT support structure. More information about each of these processes can be found in Chapter 12 of this pocket guide.

Service Operation processes:

- *Event management* - Surveys all events that occur in the IT infrastructure in order to monitor the regular performance, and which can be automated to trace and escalate unforeseen circumstances.
- *Incident management* - Focuses on restoring failures of services as quickly as possible for customers, so that it has a minimal impact on the business. Incidents can for example be failures, questions or queries.
- *Problem management* - Includes all activities needed for a diagnosis of the underlying cause of incidents, and to determine a resolution for those problems.
- *Request fulfillment* - The process of dealing with service requests from the users, providing a request channel, information, and delivery of fulfillment of the request.
- *Access management* - The process of allowing authorized users' access to use a service, while access of unauthorized users is prevented.

Service Operation activities:

- *Monitoring and control* - Based on a continual cycle of monitoring, reporting and undertaking action. This cycle is crucial to providing, supporting and improving services.
- *IT operations* - Fulfill the day-to-day operational activities that are needed to manage the IT infrastructure.
- There are a number of operational activities which ensure that the technology matches the service and process goals. For example *mainframe management, server management and support, network management, database management, directory services management, and middleware management.*
- *Facilities and data centre management* refers to management of the physical environment of IT operations, which are usually located in computing centers or computer rooms. Main components of facilities management are for example building management, equipment hosting, power management and shipping and receiving.

6.4   Organization

Service Operation has some logical functions (see also Chapter 8) that deal
with service desk, Technical Management, IT Operations Management
and Application Management:

- A *service desk* is the Single Point of Contact (SPOC) for users, dealing
  with all incidents, access requests and service requests. The primary
  purpose of the service desk is to restore "normal service" to users as
  quickly as possible.
- *Technical Management* refers to the groups, departments or teams
  that provide technical expertise and overall management of the IT
  infrastructure. Technical Management plays a dual role. It is the
  custodian of technical knowledge and expertise related to managing the
  infrastructure. But it is also provides the actual resources so support the
  ITSM lifecycle.
- *IT Operations Management* executes the daily operational activities
  needed to manage the IT infrastructure, according to the performance
  standards defined during Service Design. IT Operations Management
  has two functions: IT Operations Control, which ensures that routine
  operational tasks are carried out, and Facilities Management, for the
  management of physical IT environment, usually data centres or
  computer rooms.
- *Application Management* is responsible for managing applications in
  their lifecycle. Application Management also plays an important role
  in the design, testing and improvement of applications that are part of
  IT services. One of the key decisions in Application Management is
  whether to buy an application that supports the required functionality,
  or whether to build the application self according to the organization's
  requirements.

Roles and responsibilities within Service Operation include:

- Service desk manager
- Service desk supervisor

- Service desk analysts
- Super users
- Technical managers/Team leaders
- Technical analysts/Architects
- Technical operators
- IT operations manager
- Shift leader
- IT operations analysts
- IT operators
- Application Managers and Team Leaders
- Application Analysts and Architects
- Incident manager
- Problem manager
- Contract manager
- Building manager

There are several ways to organize Service Operation functions, and each organization will come to its own decisions based on its size, geography, culture and business environment.

6.5   Methods, techniques and tools

The most important requirements for Service Operation are:
- an integrated IT Service Management technology (or toolset) with the following core functionality:
  - self-help (e.g. FAQ's on a web interface)
  - workflow or process management engine
  - an integrated Configuration Management System (CMS)
  - technology for detection, implementation and licenses
  - remote control
  - diagnostic utilities
  - reporting capabilities

- dashboards
- integration with business service management

6.6   Implementation and operation

There are some general implementation guidelines for Service Operation:

- *Managing changes in Service Operation* - Service Operation staff must implement changes without negative impact on the stability of offered IT services.

- *Service Operation and Project Management* - There is a tendency not to use Project Management processes when they would in fact be appropriate. For example, major infrastructure upgrades, or the deployment of new procedures are significant tasks where Project Management can be used to improve control and manage costs and resources.

- *Determining and managing risks in Service Operation* - In a number of cases, it is necessary that risk evaluation is conducted swiftly, in order to take appropriate action. This is especially necessary for potential changes or known errors, but also in case of failures, projects, environmental risks, vendors, security risks and new clients that need support.

- *Operational staff in Service Design and Transition* - Service Operation staff should be particularly involved in the early stages of Service Design and Transition. This will ensure that the new services will actually work in practice and that they can be supported by Service Operation staff.

- *Planning and implementation of service management technologies* -There are several factors that organizations must plan before and during implementation of ITSM support tools, such as licenses, implementation, capacity checks and timing of technology/ implementation.

For a successful Service Operation, several challenges need to be overcome, such as:

- Lack of involvement among Development and Project staff.
- Justifying the financing.
- Challenges for Service Operation Managers, for example ineffective Service Transition may hamper the transition from design to production, the use of virtual teams, and the balance between the many internal and external relationships.

There are some Critical Success Factors:

- management support
- defining champions
- business support
- hiring and retaining staff
- service management training
- appropriate tools
- test validity
- measuring and reporting

Risks to successful Service Operation include:

- insufficient financing and resources
- loss of momentum in implementation Service Operation
- loss of important staff
- resistance to change
- lack of management support
- suspicion of Service Management by both IT and the business
- changing expectations of the customer

7 Lifecycle Phase: Continual Service Improvement

7.1 Introduction

Nowadays, IT departments must continually improve their services in order to remain appealing to the business. This is placed within the lifecycle phase of Continual Service Improvement (CSI). In this phase, measuring and analyzing are essential in identifying the services that are profitable and those that need to improve.

CSI should be applied throughout the entire service lifecycle, in all phases from Service Strategy to Service Operation. This way, it becomes an inherent part of both developing and delivering IT services.

CSI mainly measures and monitors the following matters:
- *Process compliance* - Are the new or modified processes being followed?
- *Quality* - Do the various process activities meet their goals?
- *Performance* - How efficient is the process?
- *Business value of a process* - Does the process make a difference?

It is recommended to implement CSI with help of frameworks specialized in quality improvement, such as the European Foundation for Quality Management Excellence Model or the Malcolm Baldrige National Quality Award.

7.2   Basic concepts

Organizational change is needed to make continual improvement a permanent part of the organizational culture. John P. Kotter, Professor of Leadership at the Harvard Business School, discovered eight crucial steps to successful organizational change:

- create a sense of urgency
- form a leading coalition
- create a vision
- communicate the vision
- empower others to act on the vision
- plan for and create quick wins
- consolidate improvements and create more change
- institutionalize the changes

In the 1930s, the American statistician Deming developed a step-by-step improvement approach: the *Plan-Do-Check-Act Cycle (PDCA)*:

- *Plan* - What needs to happen, who will do what and how?
- *Do* - Execute the planned activities.
- *Check* - Check whether the activities yield the desired result.
- *Act* - Adjust the plan in accordance to the checks.

These steps are followed by a consolidation phase to engrain the changes into the organization. The cycle is also known as the Deming Cycle (Figure 7.1).

CSI uses the PDCA Cycle in two areas:

- *Implementation of CSI* - Plan, implement (do), monitor, measure, and evaluate (check) and adjust (act) CSI.
- *Continual improvement of services and processes* - This area focuses on the "check" and "act" phase, with few activities in the "plan" and "do" phase, such as setting goals.

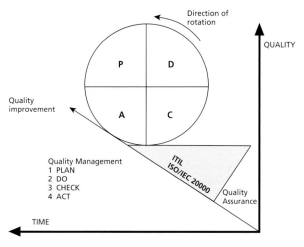

Figure 7.1 PDCA Cycle

A *metric* measures whether a certain variable meets its set target. CSI needs three types:

- *Technology metrics* - Performance and availability of components and applications.
- *Process metrics* - Performance of service management processes.
- *Service metrics* - End service results, measured by component metrics.

Define *Critical Success Factors (CSFs)*: elements essential to achieving the business mission. KPIs following from these CSFs determine the quality, performance, value, and process compliance. They can either be *qualitative* (customer satisfaction), or *quantitative* (costs of a printer incident).

Metrics supply quantitative *data*. CSI transforms these into qualitative *information*. Combined with experience, context, interpretation and reflection this becomes *knowledge*. The CSI improvement process focuses on the acquirement of *wisdom*: being able to make the correct assessments and the correct decisions by using the data, information and knowledge in the best possible way. This is called the *data-information-knowledge-wisdom* model (DIKW).

Governance drives organizations and controls them. *Corporate governance* provides a good, honest, transparent and responsible management of an organization. *Business governance* results in good company performances. Together they are known as *enterprise governance*. See Figure 7.2. *IT governance* is part of enterprise governance and comprises both corporate governance and business governance.

CSI policies capture agreements about measuring, reporting, CSFs, KPIs and evaluations.

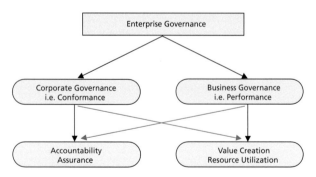

Figure 7.2 The enterprise governance framework (Source: CIMA)

7.3   Processes and other activities

This section briefly explains the processes and activities of a Continual Service Improvement. More information about each of these processes can be found in Chapter 13 of this pocket guide.

Before you start with an improvement process, you should set the direction, using the CSI model:

1. *What is the vision?* - Formulate a vision, mission, goals and objectives together with the business.
2. *Where are we now?* - Record the current situation and set the baseline.
3. *Where do we want to be?* - Determine measurable targets.
4. *How do we get there?* - Draw up a detailed Service Improvement Plan (SIP).
5. *Did we get there?* - Measure whether the objectives have been achieved, and check whether the processes are complied with.
6. *How do we keep the momentum going?* - Engrain the changes in order to maintain them.

Continual Service Improvement processes:
- *The CSI improvement process* (or 7-step improvement process) - Describes how you should measure and report.
- *Service reporting* - Reports on results and service level developments.

Continual Service Improvement activities:
- *Service measurement* - Determines the value of the services with regard to the agreed service levels.

7.4   Organization

Besides temporary roles such as project managers, CSI describes the following permanent roles:
- Service manager
- CSI manager
- Service knowledge manager
- Service owner
- Process owner
- Reporting analysts

7.5   Methods, techniques and tools

There are various methods and techniques to check whether planned improvements actually produce measurable improvements:

- *Implementation review* - Evaluates whether the improvements produce the desired effects.
- *Assessment* - Compares the performance of a process or organization against a performance standard, such as an SLA or a maturity standard.
- *Benchmark* - A special type of assessment: organizations compare (parts of) their processes with the performance of the same types of processes that are commonly recognized as "best practice".
- *Gap Analysis* - Determines where the organization is now and the size of the gap with where it wants to be.
- *Balanced Scorecard* - Includes four different perspectives on organizational performance: customer, internal processes, learning and growth and financial.
- *SWOT-analysis* - Looks at the Strengths, Weaknesses, Opportunities and Threats of an organization or component.
- *Rummler-Brache swim-lane diagram* - Visualizes the relationships between processes and organizations or departments with "swim lanes". Swim lanes are strong tools for communication with business managers, as they describe a process from an organizational viewpoint, and this is the way most managers look at a process.

Mostly, one method or technique is not enough: try to find the best mix for your organization.

CSI needs different types of software to support, test, monitor and report on the ITSM processes. The requirements for enhancing tools need to be established and documented in the answer to the question: 'Where do we want to be?'

7.6 Implementation and operation

Before you implement CSI you must establish:

- roles for trend analysis, reporting and decision-making
- a testing and reporting system with the appropriate technology
- services are evaluated internally before the IT organization discusses the test results with the business

The *business case* must clarify whether it is useful to start with CSI. On the basis of a set *baseline* an organization can compare the *benefits* and *costs* of the present situation with the benefits and costs of the improvement. Costs may be related to labor, training and tools.

Benefits of CSI may be:

- shorter time to market
- customer bonding
- lower maintenance costs

Critical Success Factors for CSI include:

- adoption by the whole organization, including the senior management
- clear criteria for the prioritization of improvement projects
- technology to support improvement activities

Introduction of CSI comes with the following challenges and risks:

- too little knowledge of the IT impact on the business and its important processes
- neglecting the information from reports
- insufficient resources, budget and time
- trying to change everything at once
- resistance against (cultural) changes
- poor supplier management
- lack of sufficient testing of all improvement aspects (people, process and products)

CSI uses a lot of data from the entire Service Lifecycle and virtually all its processes. CSI thus gains insight into the improvement opportunities of an organization.

Service level management, from the Design phase of the Lifecycle, is the most important process for CSI. It discusses with the business what the IT organization needs to measure and what the results should be. SLM maintains and improves the quality of IT services by constantly agreeing, monitoring and reporting on IT service levels.

As with all other changes in the Lifecycle, CSI changes must go through the change, release, and deployment process. CSI must therefore submit a *Request for Change* (RFC) with change management and conduct a *Post Implementation Review* (PIR) after implementation. The CMDB should be updated as well.

PART 2
ITIL FUNCTIONS AND PROCESSES

8 Introduction to Functions and Processes

This chapter provides an overview of the basic concepts of the functions and processes that are included in the five phases of the Service Lifecycle.

Processes and functions are defined as follows:

- *Process* - A structured set of activities designed to accomplish a defined objective. Processes have inputs and outputs, result in a goal-oriented change, and utilize feedback for self-enhancing and self-corrective actions. Processes are measurable, provide results to customers or stakeholders, are continual and iterative and are always originating from a certain event. Processes can run through several organizational units. An example of a process is change management.
- *Function* - A team or group of people and the tools they use to carry out one or more processes or activities, specialized in fulfilling a specified type of work, and responsible for specific end results. Functions have their own practices and their own knowledge body. Functions can make use of various processes. An example of a function is a service desk. (Note: "function" can also mean "functionality", "functioning", or "job".)

We can study each process separately to optimize its quality:

- The *process owner* is responsible for the process results.
- The *process manager* is responsible for the realization and structure of the process, and reports to the process owner.
- The *process operatives* are responsible for defined activities, and these activities are reported to the process manager.

The management of the organization can provide control on the basis of data from the results of each process. In most cases, the relevant performance indicators and standards will already be agreed upon, and the process manager can do the day-to-day control of the process. The process owner will assess the results based on a report of performance indicators and checks whether the results meet the agreed standard. Without clear indicators, it would be difficult for a process owner to determine whether the process is under control, and if planned improvements are being implemented.

Processes are often described using procedures and work instructions:

- A *procedure* is a specified way to carry out an activity or a process. A procedure describes the "how", and can also describe "who" executes the activities. A procedure may include stages from different processes. Procedures will vary depending on the organization.
- A set of *work instructions* defines how one or more activities in a procedure should be executed in detail, using technology or other resources.

When setting up an organization, positions and roles are also used, in addition to the various groups (teams, departments, divisions):

- *Roles* are sets of responsibilities, activities and authorities granted to a person or team. One person or team may have multiple roles; for example, the roles of Configuration Manager and Change Manager may be carried out by one person.
- *Job positions* are traditionally recognized as tasks and responsibilities that are assigned to a specific person. A person in a particular position has a clearly defined package of tasks and responsibilities which may include various roles. Positions can also be more broadly defined as a logical concept that refers to the people and automated measures that carry out a clearly defined process, an activity or a combination of processes

or activities. Individuals and roles have an N:N relationship (many-to-many).

People, process, products and partners (the four Ps) provide the main "machinery" of any organization, but they only work well if the machine is oiled: *communication* is an essential element in any organization. If the people do not know about the processes or use the wrong instructions or tools, the outputs may not be as anticipated. Formal structures on communication include:

- *Reporting* - Internal and external reporting, aimed at management or customers, project progress reports, alerts.
- *Meetings* - Formal project meetings, regular meetings with specific targets.
- *Online facilities* - Email systems, chat rooms, pagers, groupware, document sharing systems, messenger facilities, teleconferencing and virtual meeting facilities
- *Notice boards* - Near the coffee maker, at the entrance of the building, in the company restaurant.

It is recommended that a common understanding of processes, projects, programs, and even portfolios is created. The following definitions may be used:

- *Process* - A process is a structured set of activities designed to accomplish a defined objective.
- *Project* - A project is a temporary organization, with people and other assets required to achieve an objective.
- *Program* - A program consists of a number of projects and activities that are planned and managed together to achieve an overall set of related objectives.
- *Portfolio* - A portfolio is a set of projects and/or programs, which are not necessarily related, brought together for the sake of control, coordination and optimization of the portfolio in its totality. NB: A

Service Portfolio is the complete set of services that are managed by a service provider.

8.1   ITIL V3 Lifecycle Clustering

ITIL V3 contains five core books - one for each phase of the Lifecycle. Each of the five Lifecycle phases describes processes, functions and "miscellaneous activities". This lifecycle classification represents another dimension than the process structure, which describes the service provider's operating method. As such, a process generally occurs in multiple phases.

The detailed description of a process or function is included in just one of the five books, even if the process is just as relevant in other phases (books). In this case, the book in which the process or function makes its main contribution to the lifecycle is selected.

The processes and functions described in this chapter are listed in ITIL order below:

Service Strategy
1.   Financial management
2.   Service portfolio management
3.   Demand management

Service Design
4.   Service catalogue management
5.   Service level management
6.   Capacity management
7.   Availability management
8.   IT service continuity management
9.   Information security management
10. Supplier management

Service Transition

11. Transition planning and support
12. Change management
13. Service asset & configuration management
14. Release and deployment management
15. Service validation and testing
16. Evaluation
17. Knowledge management

Service Operation

18. Event management
19. Incident management
20. Request fulfillment
21. Problem management
22. Access management
23. Monitoring and control
24. IT operations
25. Service desk

Continual Service Improvement

26. The 7-step improvement process (CSI Improvement Process)
27. Service reporting

The next chapters show these processes and functions in the various Lifecycle phases.

9 Functions and Processes in Service Strategy

9.1 Financial Management

Introduction

Financial management is an integrated component of service management. It provides vital information that management needs to guarantee efficient and cost-effective service delivery. If strictly implemented, financial management generates meaningful and critical data on performance. It is also able to answer important organization issues, such as:

- Does our differentiation strategy result in higher profits and revenue, reduced costs or increased coverage?
- Which services cost most and why?
- Where are our greatest inefficiencies?

Financial management ensures that the charges for IT services are transparent via the Service Catalogue and that the business understands them. The benefits are:

- improved decision-making
- inputs for Service Portfolio Management
- financial compliance and control
- operational control
- value capture and creation

Basic concepts

Two vital value concepts for service valuation are defined:

- *Provisioning value* - The actual underlying costs of IT (creation costs), both tangible and intangible. Examples of these costs include: hardware and software license costs, annual maintenance costs, facility costs, taxes, compliance costs.

- *Service value potential* - The value-adding component based on the customer's value perception or the expected additional utility and warranty that the customers can obtain compared to their own assets. Look at the service's individual value components to determine the true value of the service. Determine the eventual value of the service by adding these components and comparing them against the costs (provisioning value).

Financial Management ensures correct funding for the purchase and the delivery of services. The expected demand for IT services is qualified and translated into financial terms via a plan. This plan may have three primary areas, each of which delivers financial results that are necessary for continued transparency and service valuation:

- *Operating & capital planning* (general and fixed asset ledgers) - Translation of IT expenditures to collective financial systems as part of the collective planning cycle.
- *Demand planning* - Need for and use of IT services as described earlier.
- *Regulatory and environmental planning* (compliance) - Is driven from the business.

Financial management acts as a bridge between collective financial systems and service management systems. A service-oriented accounting function results in far more detail and understanding of the delivery and consumption of services, as well as the production of data for the planning process. Related functions and accounting properties are:

- *Service recording* - Allocating a cost center for a service.
- *Cost types* - High-level expenses, such as hardware, software, personnel costs, administration.
  - Once the basis for cost administration (e.g. per department, service or customer) is established, cost types are determined for cost entry.

- The number of cost types can vary depending on the organization's size.
- Cost types must have a clear and recognizable description, so that costs can be easily allocated.
- The cost types can then be split up into cost items and settlement for each cost item may be established at a later stage.
- *Cost classification* - To ensure good cost control, it is important to gain insight into the types of costs that occur. Costs can be split up according to various aspects.

Variable Cost Dynamics (VCD) analyzes and searches for insight into the many variables that have an impact on the service costs. The VCD analysis is able to determine the expected impact of events like acquisitions, divestments and changes in the Service Portfolio or service alternatives.

Activities

During service valuation activities, the following decisions are made:
- *Direct costs versus indirect costs* - Can costs be attributed directly to a specific service or are they shared by several services (indirect costs)? Once the depth and width of the cost components have been identified, rules or policy plans may be required to indicate how the costs must be spread across the services.
- *Labor costs* - Develop a system to calculate the wage costs for a certain service.
- *Variable costs* - Variable expenses that depend on e.g. the number of users or the number of occurring events. To predict variable costs, you can use:
  - <u>Tiers</u> - Identify price breaks to encourage customers to buy a specific volume that is efficient to the customer and provider.
  - <u>Maximum costs</u> - Describe the costs of a service based on maximum variation.

- <u>Average costs</u> - Set the costs at an average calculated over a defined period.
- *Translation of cost account data to service value* - Can be done only if the costs are linked to services.

After having established the fixed and variable costs for each service, the variable cost drivers and variation level of a service should be determined.

Traditional models to fund IT services include:
- *Rolling plan funding* - A constant funding cycle; suitable for a Service Lifecycle for which a funding obligation is incurred at the start of a cycle and continues until changes occur or the cycle ends.
- *Trigger based plans* - Critical triggers activate planning for a specific event; the change management process, for instance, could act as a trigger for the planning process for all approved changes that have financial consequences.
- *Zero based funding* - Only include the actual costs of a service.

The *Business Impact Analysis* (BIA) represents the basis for planning business continuity. BIA identifies the financial and operational impact that may result from an interruption of business operations as well as the impact on assets and customers. This information can help shape and improve operational performance. This is because it enables improved decision-making with regard to prioritization of incident handling, the focus of problem management, change management and release and deployment management, and project prioritization. BIA offers an additional tool to determine the costs of service failure and the relative value of a service. The costs of a service failure consist of the value of lost productivity and income for a specific period.

Some concepts in financial management have a big impact on the development of service strategies. A number of these are highlighted,

allowing each organization to determine which the best alternatives are for
its Service Strategy:

* *Cost Recovery, Value Center, or Accounting Center?* - IT's financial cycle
  starts with investment in resources that create the outputs. Customers
  identify that outputs as value, reinitiating the cycle. Depending on the
  acknowledgement of the added value, IT is then considered a cost center
  or a valuable asset for the business objectives.
* *Chargeback: to charge or not to charge?* - A chargeback model for IT
  can enable justification and transparency. Charging costs increases the
  customer organization's awareness of the costs incurred to provide it
  with information. There are several chargeback models:
  - *Notional charging* - An accounting method that provides insight into
    the costs that would be charged for a specific settlement method.
  - *Metered usage* - Settling costs on the basis of carefully established
    consumption units; applies exclusively for organizations that have
    made serious progress in introducing financial management.
  - *Direct plus* - Less complex settlement model in which the allocated
    direct costs of a service are increased by a percentage of the general
    indirect costs for shared services.
  - *Fixed or user cost* - Simplest settlement model in which the costs are
    divided on the basis of an accepted computing factor, such as the
    number of users; this method does not allow for much distinction
    and therefore makes the least contribution to cost awareness.
* *Financial Management implementation checklist* - A number of example
  implementation steps for phased implementation: plan, analyze, design,
  implement, measure.

Inputs/Outputs
Financial Management gathers data inputs from the whole organization
and helps to generate and disseminate information as an output to base
critical decisions and activities on.

9.2   Service Portfolio Management

Introduction

A Service Portfolio describes the services of a provider in terms of business value. It is a dynamic method used to govern investments in service management across the enterprise, in terms of financial values. With Service Portfolio Management (SPM), managers are able to assess the quality requirements and accompanying costs.

The goal of service portfolio management is to realize maximum value while managing risks and costs.

Basic concepts

By functioning as the basis of the decision framework, the Service Portfolio helps to answer the following strategic questions:
- Why should a client buy these services?
- Why should a client buy these services from us?
- What are the price and charge back models?
- What are our strong and weak points, our priorities and our risks?
- How should our resources and capabilities be allocated?

With an efficient portfolio having optimal ROI and risk levels, an organization can maximize the value realization on its constrained and limited resources and capabilities.

Product managers play an important role in the service portfolio management. They are responsible for managing services as a product during the entire lifecycle. Product managers coordinate and focus the organization and own the Service Catalogue. They work closely together with the Business Relationship Managers, who coordinate and focus on the Client Portfolio. In essence, SPM is a Governance method.

The Service Portfolio covers three subsets of services:
- *Service Catalogue* - That part of the Service Portfolio that is visible to customers. The Service Catalogue is an essential strategy tool because it can be viewed as the virtual projection of the actual and available capabilities of the service provider.
- *Service Pipeline* - Consists of all services that are either under consideration or in development for a specific market or customer. These services are to be applied in the production phase via the Service Transition phase. The pipeline represents the growth and strategic anticipation for the future.
- *Retired Services* - Services that are phased out or withdrawn. The phasing out of services is a component of Service Transition and is necessary to guarantee that all agreements with customers will be kept.

Activities

SPM is a dynamic and continuous process that entails the following work methods (see also Figure 9.1):
- *Define* - Making an inventory of services, business cases and validating the portfolio data; start with collecting information on all existing and proposed services in order to determine the costs of the existing portfolio; the cyclic nature of the SPM process signifies that this phase does not only make the inventory of the services, but also validates the data over and over again; each service in the portfolio should have a business case.
- *Analyze* - Maximizing the portfolio value, tuning, prioritizing and balancing supply and demand; in this phase, the strategic goals are given a concrete form. Start with a series of top/down questions such as: What are the long-term goals of the service organization? Which services are required to realize these goals? Which capabilities and resources are necessary to attain these services? The answers to these questions form the basis of the analysis, but also determine the desired result of SPM.

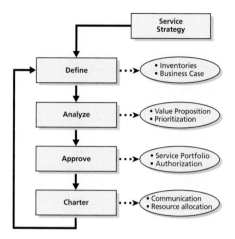

Figure 9.1 Service portfolio management

Service investments must be subdivided into three strategic categories:
- *Run the Business* - RTB investments concentrate on maintaining the service production.
- *Grow the Business* - GTB investments are intended to expand the scope of services.
- *Transform the Business* - TTB investments are meant to move into new market spaces.
- *Approve* - Finishing the proposed portfolio, authorizing services and resources and making decisions for the future. There are six different outcomes: retain, replace, rationalize, refactor, renew and retire.
- *Charter* - Communicating decisions, allocating resources and chartering services. Start with a list of decisions and action items and communicate these clearly and unambiguously to the organization. Decisions must be in tune with the budget decisions and financial plans. New services proceed to the Services Design Phase and existing services are renewed in the Service Catalogue.

Inputs/Outputs

Financial Management is a key *input* to Service Portfolio Management. By understanding cost structures applied in the provisioning of a service, service costs can be benchmarked against other providers. This IT financial information can be used together with service demand and internal capability information. This way, beneficial decisions can be made regarding whether a certain service should be provisioned internally (the *output*).

Service Portfolio Management provides input for the refreshing services in the Service Catalogue.

9.3   Demand Management

Introduction

Demand management is a vital aspect of service management. It aligns supply with demand and aims to predict the sale of products as closely as possible and, if possible, even regulate it.

Service management must deal with the additional problem of synchronous production and consumption. Service Operation is impossible without the existence of a demand that consumes the product. It is a pull-system, in which consumption cycles stimulate the production cycles (Figure 9.2).

It is therefore not possible to produce service output and store it until demand arises. The production capacity of the resources available for a service is therefore adjusted in accordance with demand prognoses and patterns.

Activity-based demand management: business processes are the primary source of demand for services. Patterns of Business Activity (PBAs) have an impact on demand patterns.

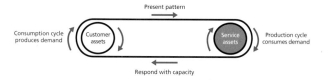

Figure 9.2 Close relationship between demand and capacity

It is extremely important to study the customer's business and thus identify, analyze and record patterns. This creates a sufficient basis for capacity management.

Basic concepts

- *Service packages* - A service package is a detailed description of an IT
  service that can be delivered to customers. A service package consists
  of a Service Level Package (SLP) and one or more core services and
  supporting services.
- *Service Level Package (SLP)* - A defined level of utility and warranty for a
  particular Service Package, from the perspective of the user. Each SLP is
  designed to meet the needs of a particular Pattern of Business Activity.
- *Core Service Package (CSP)* - A detailed description of a core service that
  may be shared by two or more Service Level Packages.
- *Line of Service (LOS)* - A core service or supporting service that has
  multiple Service Level Packages. A Line of Service is managed by a
  Product Manager and each Service Level Package is designed to support
  a particular market segment.

Activities

Core services deliver the basic results to the customer. They represent the
value that customers require and for which they are willing to pay. Core
services represent the basis for the value-proposition to the customer.
Supporting services enable that value proposition (enabling services or
Basic Factors) or improve it (Enhancing services or Excitement Factors).

Bundling core services and supporting services are a vital aspect of a
market strategy. Service providers should thoroughly analyze the prevailing
conditions in their business environment, the needs of the customer
segments or types they serve, and the alternatives that are available to these
customers. These are strategic decisions - they shape a long-term vision that
is intended to enable the organization to create lasting value for customers,
even if the methods, standards, technologies and regulations in an industry
change. Bundling supporting services with core services affects Service
Operations and represents challenges for the Design, Transition and CSI
(Continual Service Improvement) phases.

Service providers must focus on the effective delivery of value through core services, while at the same time keeping an eye on the supporting services. Research has shown that customers are often dissatisfied with supporting services. Some supporting services, such as the helpdesk or technical support, are generally bundled but can also be offered separately. This is an important consideration in the strategic planning and review of the plans. These strategic decisions can have a major impact on the service provider's success at the portfolio level. They are important primarily to service providers who supply multiple organizations or business units (BU's) while at the same time being forced to reduce costs in order to preserve the competitiveness of their portfolio.

Inputs/Outputs

Business processes are the primary inputs for demand management. Patterns of Business Activity (PBAs) influence the demand forecasts and patterns. Analyzing PBAs within demand management can deliver inputs to other service management processes such as:

- Service Design - To make the design suit the demand patterns.
- Service Catalogue management - To have the appropriate services available.
- Service Portfolio Management - To approve investing in additional capacity, new services, changes to services.
- Financial management - To approve suitable incentives to influence demand.

Inputs:
- resource utilization profiles of services
- PBAs

Outputs:
- financial constraints (e.g. pricing and charging policies)
- physical constraints (e.g. limited availability)

10 Functions and Processes in Service Design

10.1 Service Catalogue Management

Introduction

The purpose of Service Catalogue Management (SCM) is the development and upkeep of a Service Catalogue that contains all details, status, possible interactions and mutual dependencies of all present services and those under development.

Basic concepts

Over the years, organizations IT infrastructures grow at a steady pace. For this reason, it is difficult to obtain an accurate picture of the services offered by the organizations and whom they are offered to. To get a clearer picture, a Service Portfolio is developed (with a Service Catalogue as part of it), and kept up-to-date. The development of the Service Portfolio is a component of the Service Strategy phase.

It is important to make a clear distinction between the Service Portfolio and the Service Catalogue:

- *Service Portfolio* - The Service Portfolio contains information about each service and its status. As a result, the Portfolio describes the entire process, starting with the client requirements for the development, building and execution of the service. The Service Portfolio represents all active and inactive services in the various phases of the lifecycle.
- *Service Catalogue* - The Service Catalogue is a subset of the Service Portfolio and only consists of active and approved services (at user level) in Service Operation. The Service Catalogue divides services into

components. It contains policies, guidelines and responsibilities, as well as prices, service level agreements and delivery conditions.

Many organizations integrate and maintain the Service Portfolio and Service Catalogue as a part of their Configuration Management System (CMS). By defining every service the organization can relate the incidents and Requests for Change to the services in question. Therefore changes in both Service Portfolio and Service Catalogue must be part of the change management process.

The Service Catalogue can also be used for a Business Impact Analysis (BIA) as part of IT Service Continuity Management (ITSCM), or as starting point for the re-distribution of the workload as part of capacity management. These benefits justify the investment (in time and money) involved in preparing a Catalogue and making it worthwhile.

The Service Catalogue has two aspects:
- *The Business Service Catalogue* - Contains all details of the services that are being supplied to the client, and the relations with different departments and processes that depend on the service.
- *The Technical Service Catalogue* - Contains not only the details of the services supplied to the client, but also their relation to the supporting and shared services, components and CIs. This is the part that is not visible to the client.

A combination of both aspects provides a quick overview on the impact of the incidents and changes. For this reason, many mature organizations combine both aspects in a Service Catalogue, as part of a Service Portfolio.

Activities

The Service Catalogue is the only resource which contains consistant information about all services of the service provider. The catalogue should be accessible to every authorized person. Activities include:

- Defining the services.
- Producing and maintaining an accurate Service Catalogue.
- Providing information about the Service Catalogue to stakeholders.
- Managing the interaction, mutual dependency, consistency and monitoring of the Service Portfolio.
- Managing the interaction and mutual dependency between the services and supporting services in the Service Catalogue, and monitoring the CMS.

Inputs/Outputs

Inputs:

- business information and organization plans
- IT plans and financial plans
- Business Impact Analysis (BIA)
- Service Portfolio

Outputs:

- service definition
- updates for Service Portfolio
- Service Catalogue

10.2 Service Level Management

Introduction

The objective of the Service Level Management (SLM) process is to agree on the delivery of IT services and to make sure that the agreed level of IT service provision is attained.

Basic concepts

The SLM process entails planning, coordinating, supplying, agreeing, monitoring and reporting on *Service Level Agreements* (SLAs). This also includes the ongoing review of the service rendered. This way, the quality satisfies the agreed requirements and can be improved where possible. The SLA is a written agreement between the Service Provider and a customer containing mutual goals and responsibilities. Options for SLAs are:

* *service-based SLAs*
* *customer-based SLAs*
* *multi-level SLAs*

An *Operational Level Agreement* (OLA) is an agreement betweean IT service provider and another part of the same organization. An OLA defines the goods or services to be provided from one department to the other, and the responsibilities of both parties.

An *Underpinning Contract (UC)* is a contract with a third party, in support of the delivery of an agreed IT service to a customer. The UC defines targets and responsibilities that are required to meet agreed service level targets in an SLA.

Activities

The activities of Service Level Management (Figure 10.1) are:

* *Design of SLM Frameworks* - SLM has to design the best possible SLA,

so that all services can be provided and clients can be serviced in a
manner that meets mutual needs.

• *Determining, documenting and agreeing on the requirements for new
  services and production of Service Level Requirements (SLRs)* - When the
  Service Catalogue is made and the SLA structure determined, the first
  SLR (a customer requirement for an aspect of a service) needs to be
  determined.

• *Monitoring the performance with regard to the SLA and reporting the
  outcome* - Everything incorporated into the SLA must be measurable.
  Otherwise, disputes may arise, which may result in damaging the
  confidence.

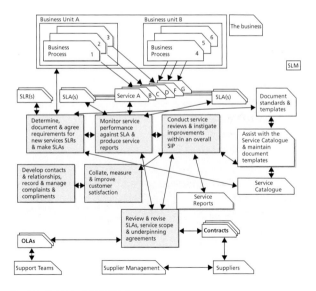

Figure 10.1 Service level management

- *Improving client satisfaction* - Besides the "hard" criteria it should also be noted how the customer experiences the service rendered, in terms of "soft" criteria.
- *Review of the underlying agreements* - The IT service provider is also dependent on its own internal technical services and external cooperation partners; in order to satisfy the SLA targets, the underlying agreements with internal departments (OLAs) and external suppliers (UCs) must support the SLA.
- *Reviewing and improving services* - Regularly consult the customer to evaluate the services and make possible improvements in the service provision; focus on those improvement items that yield the greatest benefit to the business. Improvement activities should be documented and managed in a Service Improvement Plan (SIP).
- *Developing contacts and relations* - SLM has to instill confidence in the business. With the Service Catalogue, SLM can start working proactively; the catalogue supplies information that improves the understanding of the relation between services, business units and processes.

Inputs/Outputs

Inputs:

- information arising from strategic planning
- Business Impact Analysis (BIA)
- Service Portfolio and Service Catalogue

Outputs:

- service reports
- Service Improvement Plan (SIP)
- standard document templates
- SLA, SLR and OLAs
- Service Quality Plan

10.3 Capacity Management

Introduction

Capacity management has to provide IT capacity coinciding with both the current and future needs of the customers balanced against justifiable costs. Service Strategy analyzes and decides about the wishes and requirements of customers; in the Service Design phase, capacity management is a Critical Success Factor for defining an IT service.

Basic concepts

The *Capacity Management Information System (CMIS)* provides relevant information on the capacity and performance of services in order to support the capacity management process. This information system is one of the most important elements in the capacity management process.

Activities

The capacity management process consists of:

- *reactive activities*:
  - monitoring and measuring
  - responding and reacting to capacity related events
- *proactive activities*:
  - predicting future requirements and trends
  - budgeting, planning and implementing upgrades
  - seeking ways to improve service performance
  - optimizing the performance of a service

Some activities (Figure 10.2) must be executed repeatedly (proactively or reactively). They provide basic information and triggers for other activities and processes in capacity management. For instance:

- Monitoring IT usage and response times.
- Analyzing data.
- Tuning and implementation.

Capacity management can be a extremely technical, complex and demanding process that comprises three sub-processes (Figure 10.3):

- *Business capacity management* - Translates the customer's requirements into specifications for the service and IT infrastructure; focus on current and future requirements.
- *Service capacity management* - Identifies and understands the IT services (including the sources, patterns, et cetera) to make them comply with the defined targets.
- *Component Capacity Management (CCM)* - Manages, controls and predicts the performance, use and capacity of individual IT components.

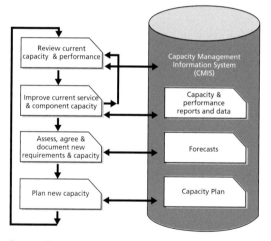

Figure 10.2 The capacity management process

All of the capacity management sub-processes analyze the information stored in the CMIS.

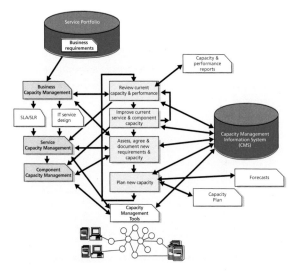

Figure 10.3 Sub-processes of capacity management

Inputs/Outputs

Inputs:

- Business information, including information from the organization plans (financial and IT-related)
- service and IT information
- change information from change management.

Outputs:

- Capacity Management Information System (CMIS)
- capacity plan (information on the current usage of the services and components)
- analyses of workload

10.4 Availability Management

Introduction

Availability management has to ensure that the delivered availability level for all services complies with or exceeds the agreed requirements in a cost-effective manner.

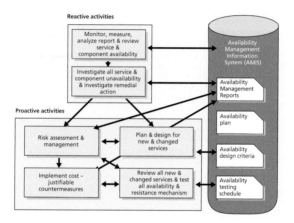

Figure 10.4 Availability management

Basic concepts

Figure 10.5 illustrates a number of starting points for availability management. The unavailability of services can be reduced by aiming to reduce each of the phases distinguished in the *extended incident lifecycle*.

Services must be restored quickly when they are unavailable to users. The *Mean Time to Restore Service (MTRS)* is the time within which a function (service, system or component) is back up after a failure. The MTRS

depends on a number of factors, such as:
- configuration of service assets
- MTRS of individual components
- competencies of support personnel
- available resources
- policy plans
- procedures
- redundancy

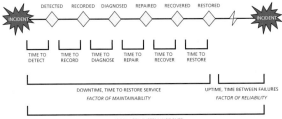

Figure 10.5 The extended incident lifecycle

Other metrics for measuring availability include:
- *Mean Time Between Failures (MTBF)* - The average time that a CI or service can perform its agreed function without interruption.
- *Mean Time Between Service Incidents (MTBSI)* - The mean time from when a system or service fails, until it next fails.
- *Mean Time To Repair (MTTR)* - The average time taken to repair a CI or service after a failure. MTTR is measured from when the CI or service fails until it is repaired. MTTR does not include the time required to recover or restore.

The *reliability* of a service or component indicates how long it can perform its agreed function without interruption.

The *maintainability* of a service or component indicates how fast it can be restored after a failure.

The *serviceability* describes the ability of a third party supplier to meet the terms of their contract, which includes agreed levels of reliability, maintainability or availability for a CI.

The reliability of systems can be increased through various types of *redundancy*.

Due to increased dependency upon IT services, customers often require services with *high availability*. This requires a design that considers the elimination of Single Points of Failure (SPOFs) and/or the provision of alternative components to provide minimal disruption to the business operation should an IT component failure occur.
High Availability solutions make use of techniques such as Fault Tolerance, resilience and fast recovery to reduce the number of incidents, and the impact of incidents.

Activities

Availability management must continuously ensure that all services comply with the objectives. New or changed services must be designed in such a way that they comply with the objectives. To realize this, availability management can perform reactive and proactive activities (Figure 10.4):

- *Reactive activities* - Executed in the operational phase of the lifecycle:
  - monitoring, measuring, analyzing and reporting the availability of services and components
  - unavailability analysis
  - expanded lifecycle of the incident
  - Service Failure Analysis (SFA)

- *Proactive activities* - Executed in the design phase of the lifecycle:
  - identifying Vital Business Functions (VBFs)
  - designing for availability
  - Component Failure Impact Analysis (CFIA)
  - Single Point of Failure (SPOF) analysis
  - Fault Tree Analysis (FTA)
  - modelling to test and analyze predicted availabilities
  - risk analysis and management
  - availability test schemes
  - planned and preventive maintenance
  - production of the Projected Service Availability (PSA) document
  - continuous reviewing and improvement

Inputs/Outputs

Inputs:
- Business information, such as organization strategies, (financial) plans and information on the current and future requirements of IT services.
- Risk analyses, Business Impact Analyses (BIA) and studies of Vital Business Functions.
- Service information from the Service Portfolio and Service Catalogue and from the SLM process.
- Change calendars and release schemas from change management and release and deployment management.

Outputs:
- the Availability Management Information System (AMIS)
- the availability plan
- availability and restore design criteria
- reports on the availability, reliability and maintainability of services

10.5 IT Service Continuity Management

Introduction

IT Service Continuity Management (ITSCM) has to support business continuity by ensuring that the required IT facilities (computer systems, networks, et cetera) can be resumed within the agreed timeframe.

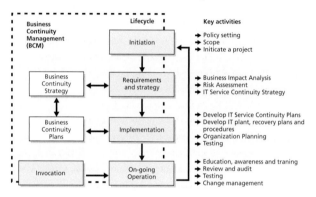

Figure 10.6 Lifecycle of IT service continuity management

Basic concepts

Once service continuity or recovery plans have been created they need to be (kept) aligned with the *Business Continuity Plans (BCPs)* and business priorities. Figure 10.6 shows the cyclic process of ITSCM and the role of overall *Business Continuity Management (BCM)*.

Activities

The process consists of four phases (Figure 10.6):

- *Initiation* - This phase covers the entire organization and includes the following activities:
  - defining the policy
  - specifying the conditions and scope

- allocating resources (people, resources and funds)
- defining the project organization and management structure
- approving project and quality plans
- *Requirements and strategies* - Determining the business requirements for ITSCM is vital when investigating how well an organization can survive a calamity. This phase includes requirements and strategy. The requirements involve the performance of a Business Impact Analysis and risk estimate:
  - <u>Requirement 1: Business Impact Analysis (BIA)</u> - Quantify the impact caused by the loss of services. If the impact can be determined in detail, it is called "hard impact" - e.g. financial losses. "Soft impact" is less easily determined. It represents, for instance, the impact on Public Relations, morale and health.
  - <u>Requirement 2: Risk estimate</u> - There are various risk analyses and methods. Risk analysis is an assessment of risks that may occur. Risk management identifies the response and counter-measures that can be taken. A standard method like Management of Risk (M_o_R) can be used to investigate and manage the risks.
  - <u>Strategy 1: Risk-reducing measures</u> - Measures to reduce risks must be implemented in combination with availability management since failure reduction has an impact on service availability. Measures may include: fault tolerant systems, good IT security controls, and off site storage.
  - <u>Strategy 2: IT recovery options</u> - The continuity strategy must weight the costs of reducing measures against the recovery measures (manual work-arounds, reciprocal arrangements, gradual recovery, intermediate recovery, fast recovery and immediate recovery) to restore critical processes.
- *Implementation* - The ITSCM plans can be created once the strategy is approved. The organization structure (leadership and decision-making processes) changes in a disaster recovery process. Set this up around a senior manager in charge.

- *Operationalization* - This phase includes:
  - education, awareness and training of personnel
  - review and audit
  - testing
  - change management (ensures that all changes have been studied for their potential impact)
  - ultimate test (invocation)

Inputs/Outputs

Inputs:

- business information (organization strategy, plans)
- IT information
- financial information
- change information (from change management)

Outputs:

- reviewed ITSCM policy
- Business Impact Analysis (BIA)
- risk analyses
- plans for disaster recovery, testing and crisis management

10.6 Information Security Management

Introduction
Information security management needs to align IT security with business security and has to ensure that information security is managed effectively in all services and service management operations.

Basic concepts
The information security management process and framework include:

- information security policy
- Information Security Management System (ISMS)
- comprehensive security strategy (related to the business objectives and strategy)
- effective security structure and controls
- risk management
- monitoring processes
- communication strategy
- training strategy

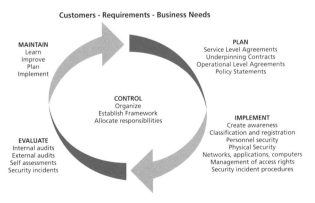

Figure 10.7 Framework for managing IT security

The ISMS represents the basis for cost-effective development of an information security program that supports the business objectives. Use the *four Ps* of People, Processes, Products (including technology) and Partners (including suppliers) to ensure a high security level where required.

The framework can be based on ISO 27001, the international standard for information security management. Figure 10.7 is based on various recommendations, including ISO 27001, and provides information about the five elements (Control, Plan, Implement, Evaluate, Maintain) and their separate objectives.

Activities

Information security management should include the following activities:
- Operation, maintenance and distribution of an information security policy.
- Communication, implementation and enforcement of security policies
- Assessment of information.
- Implementing (and documenting) controls that support the information security policy and manage risks.
- Monitoring and management of breaches and incidents.
- Proactive improvement of the control systems.

The information security manager must understand that security is not just a step in the lifecycle and that it cannot be guaranteed by technology alone. Information security is a continuous process and an integrated part of all services and systems. Figure 10.8 describes controls that can be used in the process.

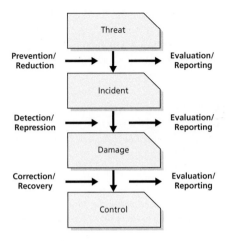

Figure 10.8 Security controls for threats and incidents

Figure 10.8 shows that a risk may result in a threat that in turn causes an incident, leading to damage. Various measures can be taken between these phases:

- *preventive measures* - prevent effects (e.g. access management)
- *reductive measures* - limit effects (e.g. backup and testing)
- *detective measures* - detect effects (e.g. monitoring)
- *repressive measures* - suppress effects (e.g. blocking)
- *corrective measures* - repair effects (e.g. rollback)

Inputs/Outputs

Inputs:

- business information (strategy, plans)
- information from the SLM process
- change information from the change management process

Outputs:

- general information security management policy
- Information security management system
- security controls, audits and reports

10.7 Supplier Management

Introduction

Supplier management has to manage suppliers and the services they supply, aiming at consistent quality at the right price.

Basic concepts

All activities in this process must result from the supplier strategy and the Service Strategy policy. Create a Supplier and Contract Database (SCD) to achieve consistency and effectiveness in implementing policy. Ideally, this database would be an integrated element of CMS or SKMS. The database should contain all details regarding suppliers and their contracts, together with details about the type of service or product, and any information and relations to other configuration items.

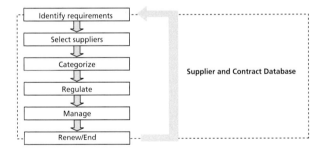

Figure 10.9 Contract Lifecycle

The data stored here will provide important information for activities and procedures such as:
- categorizing of suppliers
- maintenance of supplier and contract database
- evaluation and building of new suppliers and contracts

- building new supplier relations
- management and achievement of supplier and contract
- renewed and ended contracts

Activities

In case of external suppliers, it is recommended to draw up a formal contract with clearly defined, agreed upon and documented responsibilities and goals. Manage this contract during its entire lifecycle (Figure 10.9).

These phases are:
1. *Identify business requirements*:
   - Produce a program of requirements.
   - Provide conformity of strategy and policy.
   - Develop a business case.
2. *Evaluate and select new suppliers* - Identify new business requirements and evaluate new suppliers as part of the Service Design process. They provide inputs for all other aspects of the lifecycle of the contract. Take various issues into account when selecting a new supplier, such as references, ability, and financial aspects.
3. *Categorizing suppliers and contracts* - The amount of time and energy that should be put into a supplier depends on the impact of this supplier and its service. A subdivision could be made according to strategic relationships (managed by senior management), relationships at a tactical level (managed by middle management), execution level (execution management) and suppliers that only provide goods such as paper and cartridges.
4. *Introduce new suppliers and contracts* - In order to present a clear image of the impact of new suppliers and contracts, the change management process must add them to the Supplier and Contract Database. A Business Impact Analysis (BIA) and risk assessment, in combination with ITSCM, availability management and information security

management, could be good methods to clarify the impact of new contracts on various business units.

5. *Manage performance of suppliers and contracts* - At an operational level, the integrated processes of the client organization and of the supplier must function efficiently. Questions should be:
   - Should the supplier conform to the organization's change management process?
   - How will the service desk inform the supplier in case of incidents?
   - How will CMS information be updated when CIs change?
     During the lifecycle of the contract, keep a close eye on the following two issues in order to minimize risks:
   - the performance of suppliers
   - the services, service scope and contract reviews in comparison with original business requirements
     Make sure that provisions are still in tune with what the business initially desired.

6. *Renew or end contract* - At a strategic level, see how the contract is functioning and how relevant it will be in the future, whether changes are necessary and what the commercial performance of the contract is. Benchmarking could be an appropriate instrument to compare the current service provision with that of other suppliers in the industry. If, as a result, the decision is made to end the relationship with the supplier, it is important to assess what the consequences will be in legal and financial areas, and how the client organization and service provision will be affected.

Inputs/Outputs

Inputs:
- business information (strategy, plans)
- supplier and contract strategies
- business plan details

Outputs:

- Supplier and Contract Database (SCD)
- information about performance
- supplier improvement plans (Supplier Service Improvement Plans, SIPs)
- research reports

11 Functions and Processes in Service Transition

11.1 Transition Planning and Support

Introduction

Transition planning and support ensures the planning and coordination of resources in order to realize the specification of the Service Design. Transition planning and support plans changes and ensures that issues and risks are managed.

Basic concepts

The *Service Design Package (SDP)* that was created in the Service Design phase contains all aspects of an IT service and its requirements through each stage of its lifecycle. It includes the information about the execution of activities of the Service Transition team.

A *release* should be defined, in which the following subjects are addressed:
- naming conventions, distinguishing release types
- roles and responsibilities
- release frequency
- acceptance criteria for the various transition phases
- the criteria for leaving Early Life Support (ELS)

The following types of release can be defined:
- *Major release* - Important deployment of new hardware and software with, in most cases, a considerable expansion of the functionality.
- *Minor release* - These usually contain a number of smaller improvements; some of these improvements were previously

implemented as quick fixes but are now included integrally within a release.

- *Emergency release* - Usually implemented as a temporary solution for a problem or known error.

Activities

The activities for planning are:

1. *Set up transition strategy* - The transition strategy defines the global approach to Service Transition and the assignment of resources.
2. *Prepare Service Transition* - The preparation consists of analysis and acceptance of input from other Service Lifecycle phases and other inputs; identifying, filing and planning RFCs; monitoring the baseline and transition readiness.
3. *Plan and coordinate Service Transition* - An individual Service Transition plan describes the tasks and activities required to roll out a release in a test and production environment.
4. *Support* - Service Transition advises and supports all stakeholders. The planning and support team will provide insight for the stakeholders regarding Service Transition processes and supporting systems and tools.

Finally, Service Transition activities are monitored: the implementation of activities is compared with the way they were intended.

Inputs/Outputs

Inputs:

- authorized RFCs
- Service Design Package (SDP)
- definition of the release package and design specifications
- acceptance criteria for the service

Outputs:

- transition strategy
- integral collection of Service Transition plans

11.2 Change Management

Introduction

The primary objective of change management is to enable beneficial changes to be made, with minimum disruption to IT services. Change management ensures that changes are deployed in a controlled way, i.e. they are evaluated, prioritized, planned, tested, implemented and documented.

Changes have a proactive or reactive reason. Examples of a proactive reason are cost reduction and service improvement. Examples of reactive reasons for changes are solving service disruptions and adapting the service to a changing environment.

The change management process must:
- use standardized methods and procedures
- record all changes in the CMS
- take account of risks for the business

Basic concepts

A *Request for Change (RFC)* is a formal request to change one or more CIs.

A *normal change* is the addition, modification or elimination of an authorized, planned or supporting service (component) and its related documentation.

A *standard change* is a pre-approved, low risk and relatively common change. Standard changes must be registered by change management.

An *emergency change* is a change that must be introduced as soon as possible. For example, to repair a failure as soon as possible in an IT service that has a large negative impact on the business.

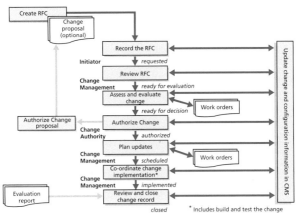

Figure 11.1 Change management

The *priority of the change* is based on impact and urgency. Change management schedules the changes on the change calendar: the Change Schedule (CS).

The *Change Advisory Board (CAB)* is a consultative body that regularly meets to help the change manager assess, prioritize and schedule the changes. In case of emergency changes, it can be necessary to identify a smaller organization to make emergency decisions: the *Emergency CAB (ECAB)*.

No change should be approved without having a remediation plan for *back out*.

A *post-implementation review (PIR)* should be carried out to determine if the change was successful and to identify opportunities for improvement.

Activities

The specific activities (see Figure 11.1) to manage individual changes are:

1. *Create and record* - An individual or department may submit an RFC. All RFCs are registered and must be identifiable.

2. *Review the RFC* - After registration, the stakeholders verify whether the RFC is illogical, unfeasible, unnecessary or incomplete, or whether it has already been submitted earlier.

3. *Assess and evaluate changes* - Based on the impact, risk assessment, potential benefits and costs of the change, the change authority determines whether a change is implemented or not.

4. *Authorize the change* - For every change there is a formal authorization required. This may be a role, person or group of people.

5. *Coordinate implementation* - Forward approved changes to the relevant product experts, so that they can build and test the changes, and create and deploy releases.

6. *Evaluate and close* - Implemented changes are evaluated after some time (*Post-Implementation Review (PIR)*). If the change is successful, it can be closed.

Inputs/Outputs

Inputs:

*   RFCs
*   change, transition, release and deployment plans
*   Change Schedule and Projected Service Outage (PSO, document that explains effects of planned changes/maintenance on service levels)
*   assets and CIs
*   evaluation report

Outputs:
- rejected or approved RFCs
- new or changed services, CIs, assets
- adjusted PSO
- updated Change Schedule
- change decisions, actions, documents, records and reports

11.3 Service Asset and Configuration Management

Introduction

Service Asset and Configuration Management (SACM) manages the service assets and Configuration Items (CIs) in order to support the other service management processes. SACM defines the service and infrastructure components and maintains accurate configuration records.

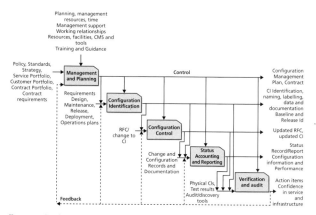

Figure 11.2 Service asset and configuration management

Basic concepts

A *Configuration Item (CI)* is an asset, service component or other item that is (or will be) controlled by configuration management.

An *attribute* is a piece of information about a CI. For example version number, name, location et cetera.

A *relationship* is a link between two CIs that identifies a dependency or connection between them. Relationships show how CIs work together to provide a service.

By maintaining relations between CIs a *logical model* of the services, assets and infrastructure is created. This provides valuable information for other processes.

A *configuration structure* shows the relations and hierarchy between CIs that comprise a configuration.

Configuration management ensures that all CIs are provided with a *baseline* and that they are maintained. A baseline can be used to restore the IT infrastructure to a known configuration if a change or release fails.

CIs are *classified* (the act of assigning a category to a CI) to help manage and trace them throughout their lifecycles, for instance: service, hardware, software, documentation, personnel.

A *Configuration Management Database* (CMDB) is a database used to store configuration records of CIs. One or more CMDBs can be part of a Configuration Management System.

In order to manage large and complex IT services and infrastructures SACM needs to use a supporting system: the *Configuration Management System (CMS)*.

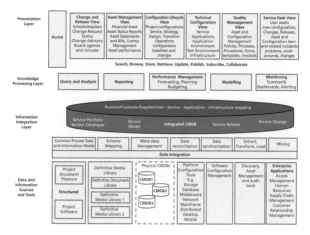

Figure 11.3 Example of a CMS

Various *libraries* are defined:

- A *secure library* is a collection of software and electronic CIs (documents) of a known type and status.
- A *secure store* is a secure location where IT assets are stored.

The *Definitive Media Library (DML)* is a secure store where the definitive, authorized (approved) versions of all media CIs are stored and monitored.

Definitive spares are spare components and assemblies that are maintained at the same level as the comparative systems within the live environment.

A *snapshot* ("moment in time") is the state of a configuration at a certain point in time (for instance when it was inventoried by a discovery tool). It can be recorded in the CMS to remain as a fixed historical record of the configuration, not necessarily authorized.

Activities

The basic SACM process activities consist of:

1. *Management and planning* - The management team and configuration management decide what level of configuration management is needed and how this level will be achieved. This is documented in a configuration management plan.

2. *Configuration identification* - Configuration identification focuses on establishing a CI classification system. Configuration identification determines: the configuration structures and selection of CIs; the naming conventions of CIs, the CI labels; relations between CIs, the relevant attributes of CIs, type of CIs et cetera.

3. *Configuration control* - Configuration control ensures that the CIs are adequately controlled. No CIs can be added, adapted, replaced or removed without following the agreed procedure.

4. *Status accounting and reporting* - The lifecycle of a component is classified into different stages. For example: development or draft, approved and withdrawn. The stages that different types of CIs go through must be properly documented and the status of each CI must be tracked.

5. *Verification and audit* - SACM conducts audits to ensure that there are no discrepancies between the documented baselines and the actual situation; and that release and configuration documentation is present before the release is rolled out.

Inputs/Outputs

Updates to assets and CIs are triggered by RFCs, service requests and incidents.

11.4   Release and Deployment Management

Introduction

Release and deployment management is aimed at building, testing and delivering the capability to provide the services specified by Service Design.

Basic concepts

A *release* is a set of new or changed CIs that are tested and will be implemented into production together.

A *release unit* is a part of the service or infrastructure that is included in the release, in accordance with the organization's release guidelines.

In the *release design* different considerations apply in respect of the way in which the release is deployed. The most frequently occurring options for the rollout of releases are: "big bang" versus phased, "push and pull", automated or manual.

A *release package* is a single release unit or (structured) collection of release units. All the elements of which the service consists - the infrastructure, hardware, software, applications, documentation, knowledge, et cetera - must be taken into account.

The *V model* (Figure 11.4) is a convenient tool for mapping out the different configuration levels at which building and testing must take place. The left side of the V in this example starts with service specifications and ends with the detailed Service Design. The right side of the V reflects the test activities, by means of which the specifications on the left-hand side must be validated. In the middle we find the test and validation criteria (See 11.5 Service validation and testing).

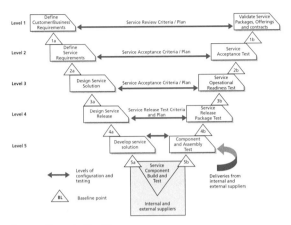

Figure 11.4 The service V model

Activities

The process activities of release and deployment management are:

1. *Planning* - Prior to a deployment into production different plans are formulated. The type and number depends on the size and complexity of the environment and the changed or new service.

2. *Preparation for building (compilation), testing and deployment* - Before approval can be given for the building and test phase, the service and release design is compared against the specifications of the new or changed service (validation).

3. *Building and testing* - The building and test phase of the release consists of the management of general (common) infrastructure and services; use of release and building documentation; acquisition, purchasing and testing of CIs and components for the release; compilation of the release (release packaging); structuring and controlling the test environments.

4. *Service testing and pilots* - Test management is responsible for the coordination of the test activities and the planning and control of the implementation. See Section 11.5 Service validation and testing.

5. *Planning and preparing the deployment* - This activity evaluates the extent to which each deployment team is prepared (readiness assessment) for the deployment.

6. *Transfer, deployment, and retirement* - The following activities are important during the deployment: the transfer of financial assets; transfer and transition of business and organization; transfer of service management resources; transfer of the service; deployment of the service; retirement of services; removal of superfluous assets.

7. *Verify deployment* - When all the deployment activities have been completed it is important to verify that all stakeholders are able to use the service as intended.

8. *Early life support* - Early Life Support (ELS) is intended to offer extra support after the deployment of a new or changed service.

9. *Review and close* - In the review of a deployment, check whether the knowledge transfer and training were adequate; all user experiences have been documented; all fixes and changes are complete and all problems, known errors and workarounds have been documented; the quality criteria have been complied with; the service is ready for transition from ELS into production.

Inputs/Outputs

Inputs:

* approved RFC, service package, SLP, SDP, continuity plans
* release policies, design and model, construction model and plan
* technology, purchasing, service management and operation standards and plans
* exit and entry criteria for each phase of the release and deployment

Outputs:

- release and deployment plans, completed RFC, service notifications, an updated Service Catalogue and service model
- new or changed service management documentation and service reports
- new tested service environment
- SLA, OLAs and contracts
- Service Transition report and service capacity plan
- Complete CI list of release package

11.5   Service Validation and Testing

Introduction

Testing of services during the service transition phase ensures that the new or changed services are *fit for purpose (utility)* and *fit for use (warranty)*.

The goal of service validation and testing is to to ensure the delivery of *that* added value that is agreed and expected. When not properly tested, additional incidents, problems and costs will occur.

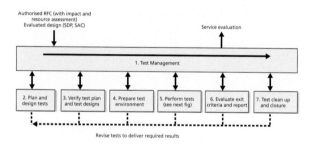

Figure 11.5 Service validation and testing

Basic concepts

The *Service Model* describes the structure and dynamics of a service provided by Service Operation. The structure consists of main and supporting services and service assets. When a new or changed service is designed, developed and built, these service assets are tested in relation to design specifications and requirements. Activities, flow of resources, coordination, and interactions describe the dynamics.

The *Test Strategy* defines the entire testing approach and the allocation of required resources.

A *Test Model* consists of a test plan, the object to be tested and test scripts which indicate the method by which each element must be tested.

The *Service Design Package (SDP)* defines *entry and exit criteria* for all test perspectives.

By using *test models*, such as a *V model* (see Figure 11.4), testing becomes a part of the Service Lifecycle early in the process.

Fit for purpose means that the service does what the client expects of it, so that the service supports the business. *Fit for use* addresses such aspects as availability, continuity, capacity and security of the service.

In addition to all kinds of functional and non-functional *test types*, *role playing* is also possible based on perspective (target group).

Activities
The following test activities can be distinguished:
- *Validation and test management* - Test management consists of planning and managing (control), and reporting on the activities taking place during all test phases of the Service Transition.
- *Planning and design* - Test planning and design activities take place early in the Service Lifecycle and relate to resources, supporting services, planning milestones and delivery and acceptance.
- *Verification of test plan and design* - Test plans and designs are verified to make sure that everything (including scripts) is complete, and that test models sufficiently take into account the risk profile of the service in question, and all possible interfaces.

- *Preparation test environment* - Prepare the test environment and make a baseline of the test environment.
- *Testing* - The tests are executed using manual or automated testing techniques and procedures. Testers register all results.
- *Evaluate exit criteria and report* - The actual results are compared with projected results (exit criteria).
- *Clean up and closure* - Make sure that the test environment is cleaned. Evaluate the test approach and determine issues that need improvement.

Inputs/Outputs

Inputs:
- the service and Service Level Package (SLP)
- interface definitions by the supplier
- Service Design Package (SDP)
- release and deployment plans
- acceptance criteria and RFCs

Outputs:
- test report, test incidents, test problems, test errors
- improvement (for CSI)
- updated data
- information and knowledge for the knowledge management system

11.6 Evaluation

Introduction

Evaluation is a generic process that is intended to verify whether the performance of "something" is acceptable; for example, whether it has the right price/quality ratio, whether it is continued, whether it is in use, whether it is paid for, and so on.

Evaluation delivers important input for Continual Service Improvement (CSI) and future improvement of service development and change management.

Basic concepts

An *evaluation report* contains a risk profile, a deviations report, a qualification and validation statement (if necessary), and a recommendation (to accept or refuse the change).

The *predicted performance* of a service is the expected performance. The *actual performance* is the performance following a service change.

Activities

The evaluation process consists of the following activities:

1. *Planning the evaluation* - When planning an evaluation, the intended and unintended effects of a change are analyzed.
2. *Evaluating the predicted performance* - Perform a risk assessment based on the customer's specifications, the predicted performance and the performance model. Send an interim assessment report to change management if the evaluation shows that the predicted performance represents an unacceptable risk to the change or deviates from the acceptance criteria. Cease the evaluation activities while awaiting a decision from change management.

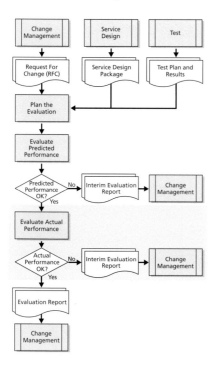

Figure 11.6 Evaluation

3. *Evaluating the actual performance* - After implementation of the service change, Service Operation reports on the actual performance of the service. Perform a second risk assessment, again based on the customer's specifications, the predicted performance and the performance model. Send a new interim assessment report to change management if the evaluation shows that the actual performance represents an unacceptable risk and cease the evaluation activities while awaiting a decision from change management.

Send an evaluation report to change management if the evaluation is approved.

Inputs/Outputs

Inputs:

- RFCs
- the Service Design Package (SDP)
- Service Acceptance Criteria (SACs)
- test plans and results

Output:

- The evaluation report

11.7 Knowledge Management

Introduction

Knowledge management improves the quality of decision-making (by the management) by ensuring that reliable and safe information is available during the Service Lifecycle.

Effective sharing of knowledge requires the development and maintenance of a Service Knowledge Management System (SKMS). This system should be available to all information stakeholders and suit all information requirements.

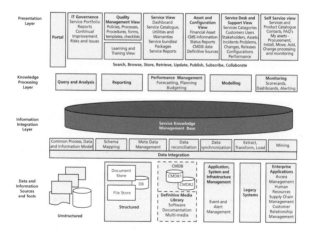

Figure 11.7 The Service Knowledge Management System

Basic concepts

Knowledge management is often visualized using the *DIKW* structure: Data-Information-Knowledge-Wisdom. Quantitative data from metrics are transformed into qualitative information. By combining information with experience, context, interpretation and reflection it becomes knowledge. Ultimately, knowledge can be used to make the right decisions which comes down to wisdom.

The basis of the *Service Knowledge Management System (SKMS)* is formed by a considerable amount of data in a central database or Configuration Management System (CMS) and the CMDB: the CMDB feeds the CMS and the CMS provides input for the SKMS and so supports the decision-making process. However, the scope of the SKMS is broader. Information is also stored that relates to matters such as:

- the experience and skills of staff
- information about peripheral issues such as the behavior of users and the performance of the organization
- requirements and expectations of suppliers and partners

There are a number of knowledge transfer techniques, such as learning styles; knowledge visualization; driving behavior; seminars; advertisements; newsletter, newspaper.

Activities

Knowledge management consists of the following activities, methods and techniques:

1. *Knowledge management strategy* - An organization needs an overall knowledge management strategy. If such a strategy is already in place, the service management knowledge strategy can link into it. The knowledge management strategy also focuses specifically on on identifying and documenting relevant knowledge, and on the data and information that support this knowledge.

2. *Knowledge transfer* - The transfer of knowledge is a challenging task that requires, in the first place, an analysis to determine what the knowledge gap is between the department or person in possession of the knowledge and those in need of the knowledge. Based on the

outcome of this analysis, a communication (improvement) plan is
formulated to facilitate the knowledge transfer.

3. *Information management* - Data and information management
    consists of the following activities: establishing data and information
    requirements; defining the information architecture; establishing
    data and information management procedures; evaluation and
    improvement.

4. *Use of the SKMS* - Supplying services to customers in different
    time zones and regions and with different operating hours imposes
    strenuous requirements on the sharing of knowledge. For this reason
    the supplier must develop and maintain an SKMS system that is
    available to all stakeholders and suits all information requirements.

Inputs/Outputs

Each organization has it own specific knowledge requirements. However,
these organizations share the requirement to manage the transfer of that
knowledge and information between phases and amongst staff.

Service delivery errors discovered during transition are recorded and
analyzed. Service Transition makes the information about the consequences
of these errors and any workarounds available to Service Operation.

Service Transition staff also collects information and data that is returned
to Service Design via CSI, and feed back information to Service Design if a
change in approach is needed.

Operations staff, like the incident management staff and first and second
line staff, is the central "collection point" for information about the day-
to-day routine of the managed services. It is essential that this information
and knowledge is documented and transferred. Staff who are working in
problem management are important users of this knowledge.

12 Functions and Processes in Service Operation

12.1 Event Management

Introduction

An event is defined as "any detectable or discernible occurrence that has significance for the management of the IT infrastructure or the delivery of IT service, and evaluation of the impact that a deviation might cause to the services."

Event management is the process that monitors all events that occur through the IT infrastructure to allow for normal operation and also to detect and escalate exceptional conditions. Event management can be automated to trace and escalate unforeseen event circumstances.

Basic concepts

Events may be classified as:

- *Events that indicate a normal operation* - For example a user logging on to use an application.
- *Events that indicate an abnormal operation* - For example a user who is trying to log on to an application with an incorrect password or a PC scan that reveals the installation of unauthorized software.
- *Events that signal an unusual but not exceptional operation* - It may provide an indication that the situation requires a little more supervision. For example utilization of a server's memory reaches within five per cent of its highest acceptable level.

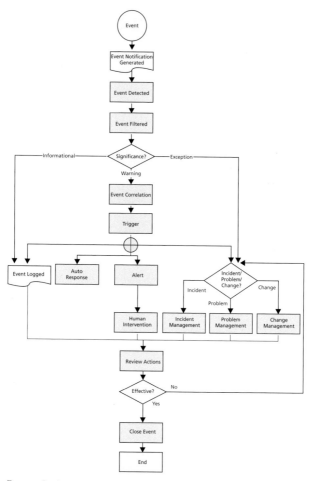

Figure 12.1 Event management

Event management can be applied to any service management aspect that must be managed and can be automated.

Activities

The main activities of the event management process are:

1. *An event occurs* - Events occur all the time, but not all of them are detected or registered. Therefore, it is important to understand what event types must be detected.
2. *Event notification* - Most CIs are designed in such a way that they communicate specific information about themselves in one of the following ways:
   – A management tool probes a device and collects specific data (this is also called "polling").
   – The CI generates a report if certain conditions are met.
3. *Event detection* - A management tool or agent detects an event report and reads and interprets it.
4. *Event filtering* - Event filtering decides whether or not the event is communicated to a management tool.
5. The *significance of events* (*event classification*) - Organizations often use their own classification to establish the importance of an event. However, it is useful to use at least the following three broad categories:
   – informative
   – alert - an alert requires a person, or team, to perform a specific action, possibly on a specific device and possibly at a specific time. For example changing a toner cartridge in a printer when the level is low.
   – exception
6. *Event correlation* - Event correlation establishes the significance of an event and determines what actions should be taken.
7. *Trigger* - If the event is recognized, a response is required. The mechanism that initiates that response is called a trigger.

8. *Response options* - The process provides a number of response options, a combination of which are allowed:
   - event logging
   - automatic response
   - alert and human intervention
   - submitting a Request for Change (RFC)
   - opening an incident record
   - opening a link to a problem record
9. *Review actions* - All important events or exceptions should be checked to determine whether they have been treated correctly, or whether event types are counted.
10. *Closing the event* - Some events remain open until specific actions have been taken.

The diagram in Figure 12.1 reflects the flow of event management.

Each event type is able to trigger event management. Among other things, triggers include:

- Exceptions at every level of CI performance established in the design specifications, Operational Level Agreements or standard processing procedures.
- An exception in a business process that is monitored by event management.
- A status change that is found in a device or database record.

Inputs/Outputs

Input:

- event notification

Outputs:
- incident record
- problem record
- Request for Change
- event record
- auto response
- alert and human intervention

12.2 Incident Management

Introduction

The incident management process handles all incidents. These may be failures, questions or queries that are reported by users (generally via a call to the service desk) or technical staff, or that are automatically detected and reported by monitoring tools.

An incident can be defined as: "an unplanned interruption to an IT service or reduction in the quality of an IT service. Failure of a CI that has not yet affected service is also an incident."

Basic concepts

With incident management, the following elements should be taken into account:

- *Timescales* - Agree on time limits for all phases and use them as targets in Operational Level Agreements (OLAs) and Underpinning Contracts (UCs).
- *Incident models* - An incident model is a way of pre-defining the steps that are necessary to handle a process (in this case, the processing of certain incident types) in an agreed way. Usage of incident models helps to ensure that standard incidents will be handled correctly and within the agreed timeframes.
- *Impact* - The effect of an incident upon business processes.
- *Urgency* - A measure of how long it will be before the incident will have a significant impact on business processes.
- *Priority* - A category for the relative importance of an incident, based on impact and urgency.
- *Major incidents* - A major incident is an incident for which the degree of impact on the user community is extreme. Major incidents require a separate procedure, with shorter timeframes and higher urgency. Agree on what defines a major incident and map the entire incident priority system.

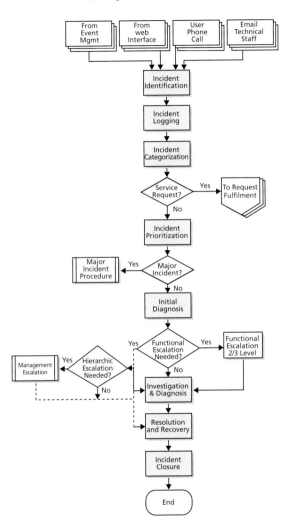

Figure 12.2 Incident management

People sometimes confuse a major incident with a problem. However, an incident always remains an incident. Its impact or priority may increase, but it never becomes a problem. A problem is the underlying cause of one or more incidents and always remains a separate entity.

Activities

The incident management process consists of the following steps (Figure 12.2):

1. *Identification* - The incident is detected or reported.
2. *Registration* - An incident record is created.
3. *Categorization* - The incident is coded by type, status, impact, urgency, SLA, et cetera.
4. *Prioritization* - Every incident gets an appropriate prioritization code to determine how the incident is handled by support tools and support staff.
5. *Diagnosis* - A diagnose is carried out to try to discover the full symptoms of the incident.
6. *Escalation* - When the service desk cannot resolve the incident itself, the incident is escalated for further support (functional escalation). If incidents are more serious, the appropriate IT managers must be notified (hierarchic escalation).
7. *Investigation and diagnosis* - If there is no known solution, the incident is investigated.
8. *Resolution and recovery* - Once the solution has been found, the issue can be resolved.
9. *Incident closure* - The service desk should check that the incident is fully resolved and that the user is satisfied with the solution and the incident can be closed.

Inputs/Outputs

Inputs:

Incidents can be triggered in many ways. The most common route is via a user who calls the service desk or completes an incident registration form in a tool or via the internet. However, many incidents are registered by event management tools more and more often.

Outputs:

• incident management reports
• RFC
• workarounds
• problem reports
• service level reports
• requests

12.3 Request Fulfillment

Introduction

The term service request is used as a general description for the various requests that users submit to the IT department. A service request is a request from a user for information, advice, a standard change, or access to a service.

For example, a service request can be a request for a password change or the additional installation of a software application on a certain work station. Because these requests occur on a regular basis and involve little risk, it is better that they are handled in a separate process. Request fulfillment (implementation of requests) processes service requests from the users.

Basic concepts

Many service requests recur on a regular basis. This is why a process flow can be devised in advance, stipulating the phases needed to handle the requests, the individuals or support groups, time limits and escalation paths involved. The service request is usually handled as a standard change.

Activities

Request fulfillment consists of the following activities, methods and techniques:

- *Menu selection* - By means of request fulfillment, users can submit their own service request via a link to service management tools.
- *Financial authorization* - Most service requests have financial implications; the cost for handling a request must first be determined; it is possible to agree on fixed prices for standard requests and give instant authorization for these requests; in all other cases the cost must first be estimated, after which the user must give permission.

- *Fulfillment* - The actual fulfillment activity depends on the nature of the service request. The service desk can handle simple requests, whereas others must be forwarded to specialist groups or suppliers.
- *Closure* - Once the service request has been completed, the service desk will close off the request.

Inputs/Outputs

Inputs:

- service requests
- Request for Change
- Service Portfolio
- security policies

Output:

- a fulfilled service request

12.4 Problem Management

Introduction

A *problem* is defined as: "the unknown cause of one or more incidents."

Problem management is responsible for the control of the lifecycle of all problems. The primary objective of problem management is to prevent problems and incidents, eliminate repeating incidents, and minimize the impact of incidents that cannot be prevented.

Basic concepts

A *root cause* of an incident is the fault in the service component that made the incident occur.

A *workaround* is a way of reducing or eliminating the impact of an incident or problem for which a full resolution is not yet available.

A *known error* is a problem that has a documented root cause and a workaround.

In addition to creating a *Known Error Database (KEDB)* for faster diagnosis, the creation of a problem model for the handling of future problems may be useful. This standard model supports the steps that need to be taken, the responsibilities of people involved and the necessary timescales.

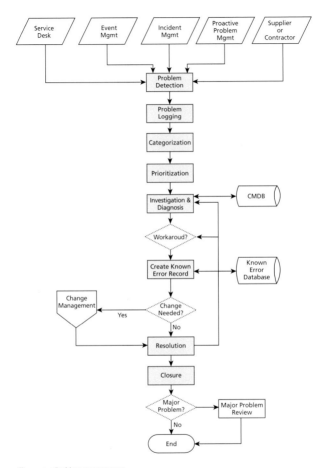

Figure 12.3 Problem management

Activities

Problem management (Figure 12.3) consists of two important processes:

- *Reactive problem management* - Analyzing and resolving the causes of incidents. Reactive problem management is performed by Service Operation.
- *Proactive problem management* - Activities to detect and prevent future problems/incidents. Proactive problem management includes the identification of trends or potential weaknesses. It is initiated by Service Operation, but usually driven by CSI (see also Chapter 13).

Inputs/Outputs

Inputs:

- problem records
- incident details
- configuration details from the configuration management database
- supplier details about the products used in the infrastructure
- Service Catalogue and Service Level Agreements
- Details about the infrastructure and the way it behaves, such as capacity records, performance measurements, Service Level reports, et cetera.

Outputs:

- problem records
- Known Error Database
- Request for Change
- closed problem records
- management information

12.5 Access Management

Introduction

Access management grants authorized users the right to use a service, and denies unauthorized users access. Some organizations also call it "rights management" or "identity management".

Access management can be initiated via a number of mechanisms, for example by means of a *service request* with the service desk.

Basic concepts

Access management has the following basic concepts:

- *Access* - Refers to the level and scope of the functionality of services or data that a user is allowed to use.
- *Identity* - Refers to the information about the people who the organization distinguishes as individuals; establishes their status in the organization.
- *Rights* - Rights are also called privileges. Refers to the actual settings for a user; the service (group) they are allowed to use. Typical rights include reading, writing, executing, editing and deleting.
- *Services or service groups* - Most users have access to multiple services; it is therefore more effective to grant every user or group of users access to an entire series of services that they are allowed to use simultaneously.
- *Directory services* - Refers to a specific type of tool used to manage access and rights.

Activities

Access management consists of the following activities:

- *Requesting access* - Access (or limitation of access) can be requested via a number of mechanisms, such as a standard request generated by the human resources department; a Request for Change (RFC), an RFC submitted via the request fulfillment process, execution of an authorized script or option.
- *Verification* - Access management must verify every access request for an IT service from two perspectives:
  - Are the users requesting access, really the person they say they are?
  - Does the user have a legitimate reason to use the service?
- *Granting rights* - Give verified users access to IT services. Access management does not decide who gets access to what IT services; it only executes the policy and rules defined by Service Strategy and Service Design.
- *Monitoring identity status* - User roles may vary over time. Changes like job changes, promotion, dismissal, retirement all influence their service needs.
- *Registering and monitoring access* - Access management does not only respond to requests; it must also ensure that the rights it has granted are used correctly.
- *Logging and tracking access* - This is why access monitoring and control must be included in the monitoring activities of all technical and application management functions as well as in all the Service Operation processes.
- *Revoking or limiting rights* - In addition to granting rights to use a service, access management is also responsible for withdrawing those rights; but it cannot make the actual decision.

Inputs/Outputs

Inputs:

- Request for Change
- service request
- request from the Human Resources (HR) department
- request from a manager or department fulfilling an HR role or who has made a decision to use a service for the first time

Outputs:

- instances of access granted by service, user, department, et cetera
- reporting on abuses of user authorizations

12.6 Monitoring and Control

Introduction

The measuring and control of services is based on a continuous cycle of monitoring, reporting and initiating action. This cycle is essential to the supply, support and improvement of services and also provides a basis for setting strategy, designing and testing services, and achieving meaningful improvement.

Basic concepts

Three terms play a leading role in monitoring and control:
- *Monitoring* - Refers to the observation of a situation to discover changes that occur over time.
- *Reporting* - Refers to the analysis, production and distribution of the outputs of the activity that is being monitored.
- *Control* - Refers to the management of the usefulness or behavior of a device, system or service. There are three conditions:
  - The action must ensure that the behavior conforms to a defined standard or norm.
  - The conditions leading to the action must be defined, understood and confirmed.
  - The action must be defined, approved and suitable for these conditions.

There are two levels of monitoring:
- *Internal monitoring and control* - Focuses on activities and items that take place within a team or department. For instance a service desk manager who monitors the number of calls to determine how many members of staff are needed to answer the telephone.
- *External monitoring and control* - Although each team or department is responsible for managing its own area, they do not act independently. Each team or department will also be controlling items and activities on

behalf of other groups, processes or functions. For example, the server management team monitors the CPU performance on important servers and keeps the workload under control. This allows essential applications to perform within the target values set by application management.

Activities

The best-known model for the description of control is the monitoring/control cycle. Although it is a simple model, it has many complex applications in IT Service Management. Figure 12.4 reflects the basic principles of control.

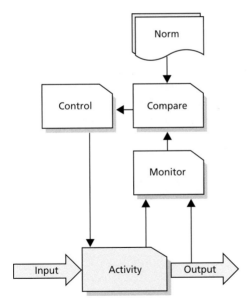

Figure 12.4 The monitoring/control cycle

The monitoring/control cycle concept can be used to manage:
- The performance of activities in a process or procedure.
- The effectiveness of the process or procedure as a whole.
- The performance of a device or a series of devices.

There are different types of monitoring tools, whereby the situation determines which type of monitoring is used:
- Active versus passive monitoring
- Reactive versus proactive monitoring
- Continuous measuring versus exception-based measuring
- Performance versus outputs

Inputs/Outputs

ITIL does not define the inputs/outputs for monitoring and control in detail. In general, anything could be monitored. However, the main issue here is the definition of monitoring and control objectives. The definition of monitoring and control objectives should ideally start with the definition of the Service Level Requirements documents. The Service Design process will help to identify the inputs for defining operational monitoring and control norms and mechanisms.

Monitoring without control is irrelevant and ineffective. Monitoring must always be aimed at achieving the service and operational objectives. Therefore, if there is no clear reason for the monitoring of a system or service, there should be no monitoring.

12.7 IT Operations

Introduction

To focus on delivering the service as agreed with the customer, the service provider will first have to manage the technical infrastructure that is used to deliver the services. Even when no new customers are added and no new services have to be introduced, no incidents occur in existing services, and no changes have to be made in existing services - the IT organization will be busy with a range of Service Operations. These activities focus on actually delivering the agreed service as agreed.

Basic concepts

The *Operations Bridge* is a central point of coordination that manages various events and routine operational activities, and reports on the status or performance of technological components.

An Operations Bridge brings together all vital observation points in the IT infrastructure so that they can be monitored and managed with minimum effort in a central location.

The Operations Bridge combines many activities, such as console management, event handling, first line network management, and support outside office hours. In some organizations, the service desk is part of the Operations Bridge.

Activities

Job scheduling: IT Operations execute standard routines, queries or reports that technical and application management teams have handed over as part of the service or as part of daily routine maintenance tasks.

Backup and restore: Essentially, backup and restore is a component of good continuity planning. Service Design must therefore ensure that there are proper backup strategies for every service. Service Transition must ensure that they are properly tested. An organization must protect its data, which includes backup and storage of data in reserved protected (and if necessary, accessible) locations.

A complete backup strategy must be agreed with the business and must cover the following elements:
- What data should the backup include, and how often must it be made?
- How many generations of data must be retained?
- The backup type and the checkpoints that are used.
- The locations used for storage and the rotation schedule.
- Transport methods that are used.
- Required tests that are used.
- Planned recovery point; the point to which data must be recovered after an IT service resumes.
- Planned recovery time; the maximum allowed time to resume an IT service after an interruption.
- How will it be checked that the backups are functional when they need to be restored?

In all cases, the IT operations staff must be qualified in backup and restore procedures. These procedures must be documented properly in the procedure manual of IT operations. Where necessary, you should include specific requirements or targets in OLAs or UCs, and specify user or customer obligations and activities in the relevant SLA.

A *restore* can be initiated from several sources, varying from an event indicating data corruption to a service request from a user or customer. A restore may be necessary in case of:

- corrupt data
- lost data
- a calamity plan / IT service continuity situation
- historical data required for forensic investigation

Many services provide their information in *print* or electronic form (*output*). The service provider must ensure that the information ends up in the right place, in the right way and in the right form. This often involves Information security.

Laws and regulations may play an important part in print and output. The archiving of important or sensitive data is particularly important.

Service providers are generally deemed to be responsible for maintaining the infrastructure to make the print and output available to the customer (printers, storage). In this case, that task must be set in the SLA.

Inputs/Outputs

Input:
- definitions of how to deliver the IT services as defined in Service Design and communicated in Service Transition

Output:
- IT services delivered to the customers

12.8 Service Desk

Introduction

A service desk is a functional unit with staff involved in differing service events. These service events come in by phone, internet or infrastructure, events which are reported automatically.

The service desk is a vitally important element of the IT department of an organization. It must be the only contact point, the Single Point of Contact (SPOC), for IT users and it deals with all incidents, access requests and service requests. The staff often uses software tools to record and manage all events.

Basic concepts

The primary purpose of the service desk is to restore "normal service" to users as quickly as possible. "Normal service" refers to what has been defined in the SLAs. This may be resolving a technical error, but also filling a service request or answering a question.

There are many ways to organize a service desk. The most important options are:

- *Local service desk* - The local service desk is located at or physically close to the users it is supporting.
- *Centralized service desk* - The number of service desks can be reduced by installing them at one single location.
- *Virtual service desk* - By using technology, specifically the internet, and by the use of support tools, it is possible to create the impression of a centralized service desk, whereas the associates are in fact spread out over a number of geographic or structural locations.

- *Follow-the-sun service* - Two or more service desks are located in different continents and combined in order to offer a 24/7 service.
- *Specialized service desk groups* - Incidents relating to a specific IT service may be routed straight to the specialized group.

Activities

Besides resuming normal service to the user as quickly as possible there are specific responsibilities for a service desk, for example:

- logging all incident/service request details
- providing first-line investigation and diagnosis
- resolving incidents/service request
- escalating incidents/service requests a service desk cannot resolve themselves within agreed timescales
- informing users about the progress
- closing all resolved incidents, requests and other calls
- updating the CMS under the direction and approval of Configuration Management if so agreed

In order to evaluate the performance of the service desk at regular time intervals, *metrics* must be established. This way, the maturity, efficiency, effectiveness and potentials can be established and the service desk actions improved.

Besides following "hard" metrics in the performance of the service desk, it is also important to carry out "soft" metrics: the Client and User Satisfaction Surveys (for example Do clients and users find that their phone calls are properly answered? Was the service desk associate friendly and professional?). Users can best complete this type of metrics, but specific questions about the service desk itself may also be asked.

Inputs/Outputs

Inputs:
- incidents
- service requests

Outputs:
- investigation and diagnoses
- resolved incidents/service requests
- escalating incidents/service requests that cannot be resolved
- keeping users informed of progress
- closing resolved incidents, requests and other calls
- communication with users
- updating the CMS

13 Functions and Processes in Continual Service Improvement

13.1 CSI Improvement Process

Introduction

The *CSI improvement process* or *7-step improvement process* describes how to measure and report on service improvement. This process is closely aligned to the PDCA Cycle and the CSI model, which should result in a *Service Improvement Plan (SIP)*. Figure 13.1 shows how the CSI model and the CSI improvement process mesh together.

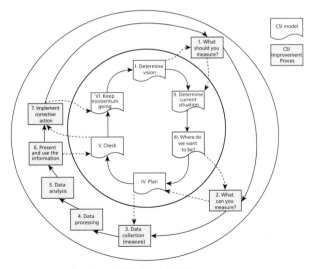

Figure 13.1 Connections between CSI Model and the CSI Improvement process

Basic concepts

Measuring is critical in CSI. It is step 3 of the CSI improvement process as discussed below. It should, however, never become a goal unto itself. Always keep in mind *why* you measure.

Before an organization can produce meaningful measurements, it needs to set its *baseline*, by answering the question "where are we now?". If there is little data available, first determine a baseline of relevant data.

Each management level should be addressed in the measuring process: strategic goals and objectives, tactical process maturity and operational metrics and KPIs. This way, a *knowledge spiral* develops: the information from Step 6 (Present and use the information) in an operational cycle is input for Step 3 (Data collection) in a tactical cycle, and information from Step 6 at the tactical level will provide data to Step 3 of a cycle at the strategic level.

Activities

CSI measures and processes measurements in a continual improvement process in seven steps:

1. *What should you measure?* - This must follow from the vision (Phase I of the CSI model) and precede the assessment of the current situation (Phase II of the CSI model).

2. *What can you measure?* - This step follows from Phase III of the CSI model: where do we want to be? By researching what the organization can measure, it will discover new business requirements and new IT options. By using a gap analysis CSI can find areas for improvement and plan these (Phase IV of the CSI model).

3. *Gather data (measure)* - In order to verify whether the organization has reached its goal (Phase V of the CSI model), it must perform measurements following from its vision, mission, goals and objectives.

4. *Process data* - The processing of data is to determine the right presentation format appropriate to each audience.
5. *Analyze data* - Discrepancies, trends and possible explanations are prepared for presentation to the business (Phase V of the CSI model).
6. *Present and use information* - The stakeholder is informed whether the goals have been achieved (still Phase V).
7. *Implement corrective action* - Create improvements, establish a new baseline and start the cycle from the top.

The cycle is preceded and closed by identification of vision and goals, which returns in Phase I of the CSI model: determine the vision.

Inputs/Outputs

The inputs for the CSI improvement process going into Step 1 consist of:
- Service Level Requirements
- Service Catalogue
- vision, mission, goals and objectives of the organization and its units
- governance requirements
- budget
- balanced scorecard
- results from SIP coming from step 7

The *output* of Step 1 is a list of what should be measured, serving as *input* for Step 2. A list of what can be measured is the *output* of Step 2. These two lists provide input for Step 3, which creates the following *output*:
- monitoring plan and procedures
- collected data concerning the ability by IT to meet business expectations
- agreement on the reliability and applicability of data

Step 4 processes this into reports and logically grouped data ready for analysis as an *output* for Step 5. *Output* from step 5 is information turned into knowledge, according to the DIKW model. Step 6, must translate knowledge into wisdom which is required to make strategic, tactical and operational decisions.

The *input*s for Step 7 are improvement opportunities suggested from Step 6. Step 7 assesses which opportunities provide the best possible outcome and implements those opportunities. This results into an SIP, which is the *output* of step 7. Measure whether desired improvements have delivered what you expected and use it as new *input* for Step 1.

13.2 Service Reporting

Introduction

The service reporting process reports on the results achieved and the developments in service levels. The aim is to convincingly support with facts any added value IT will have for the business. It should agree with the business on the layout, contents and frequency of the reports. Figure 13.2 shows how the service reporting process converts knowledge into the wisdom which is needed to make strategic, tactical and operational decisions.

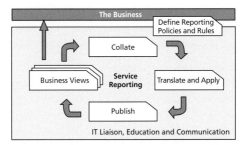

Figure 13.2 Service reporting

Basic concepts

A reporting framework is a policy that is formulated according to the rules by which you report. It should be established together with the business and Service Design, per business unit, so you can distinguish between, for example, production and sales departments. Once this has been determined, data can be translated automatically (if possible) into meaningful reports. The reporting framework should at least contain:

- target groups and their view of the services delivered
- agreement as to what should be measured and what to report
- defining all terms and upper and lower limits
- basis for all calculations
- report planning
- access to reports and media used
- meetings to discuss the reports

In order to provide useful reports to a customer, these reports should be set up from a business and end-to-end perspective. A customer is not interested in details about the functioning of the technical infrastructure through which services are provided, but only in the service itself.

Activities

The service reporting process distinguishes the following activities:

- *Gather data* - First, determine the goal and target group of the report and consider how the report is going to be used.
- *Process and apply data* - Create a hierarchical overview of the performance over the past period, focusing on events that may impact the business performance. Describe how the IT department is going to combat those threats. Also describe what went well and how IT provides value to the business.
- *Publish the information* - Publish information for the different stakeholders at all levels of the organization. Use marketing and communication techniques to reach the different target groups such as the business and IT management.
- *Tune the reporting to the business* - Consider by data group if it is valuable for the target group. Look at this from an end-to-end perspective.

Evaluate continually whether the existing reporting provides clear and unambiguous information about the performance of the IT department and adjust your reporting, if this is no longer the case.

Inputs/Outputs

The *inputs* for the reporting process are the data gathered in step 3 of the CSI improvement process. It is important to determine how the *outputs* should look like well before the inputs arrives. IT departments frequently gather large amounts of data, which are not all equally interesting to the business. Start, therefore, by determining the goal and target group of the report and consider how the report is going to be used. Is management going to read it, can managers and department heads consult it online or are you going to present the results at a meeting? What will be done with it next?

Consider your audience. The organizational level of the target group will also influence its interest for different sorts of output:

1. *Strategic Thinkers* - Strategic thinkers want short reports, with lots of attention to the risks, organization image, profitability and cost savings.
2. *Directors* - Directors want more detailed reports which summarize the development measured in time, indicating how processes support the company goals, and warning of risks.
3. *Managers and supervisors* - Managers and supervisors deal with observing the goals, team and process performance, distribution of resources and improvement initiatives. Measurements and reports must indicate how the process results are contributing to this.
4. *Team leaders and staff* - Team leaders and staff will look to emphasize the individual contribution to the company result; focus should be to fix individual metrics, acknowledge their skills and consider which training potential is available in order to involve them in the processes.

Acronyms

AMIS	Availability Management Information System
APMG	APM Group
BCM	Business Continuity Management
BCP	Business Continuity Plan
BCS	British Computer Society
BIA	Business Impact Analysis
BPO	Business Process Outsourcing
BU	Business Unit
CAB	Change Advisory Board
CCM	Component Capacity Management
CFIA	Component Failure Impact Analysis
CI	Configuration Item
CMDB	Configuration Management Database
CMIS	Capacity Management Information System
CMS	Configuration Management System
CS	Change Schedule
CSF	Critical Success Factor
CSI	Continual Service Improvement
CSP	Core Service Package
DIKW	Data Information Knowledge Wisdom
DML	Definitive Media Library
ECAB	Emergency Change Advisory Board
ELS	Early Life Support
FTA	Fault Tree Analysis
HR	Human Resources
ISMS	Information Security Management System
ITIL	Information Technology Infrastructure Library
ITSCM	IT Service Continuity Management
itSMF	IT Service Management Forum
KEDB	Known Error Database

KPI	Key Performance Indicator
KPO	Knowledge Process Outsourcing
LCS	Loyalist Certification Services
LOS	Line of Service
M_o_R	Management of Risk
MTBF	Mean Time Between Failures
MTBSI	Mean Time Between Service Incidents
MTTR	Mean Time To Repair
MTRS	Mean Time to Restore Service
OGC	Office of Government Commerce
OLA	Operational Level Agreement
PBA	Pattern of Business Activity
PDCA	Plan Do Check Act
PFS	Prerequisites for Success
PIR	Post-Implementation Review
PRINCE2	PRojects IN Controlled Environments
PSA	Projected Service Availability
PSO	Projected Service Outage
RAD	Rapid Application Development
RFC	Request for Change
SAC	Service Acceptance Criteria
SACM	Service Asset and Configuration Management
SCD	Supplier and Contract Database
SCM	Service Catalogue Management
SDP	Service Design Package
SFA	Service Failure Analysis
SIP	Service Improvement Plan
SKMS	Service Knowledge Management System
SLA	Service Level Agreement
SLM	Service Level Management
SLP	Service Level Package
SLR	Service Level Requirement

SoC	Separation of Concerns
SPM	Service Portfolio Management
SPOC	Single Point of Contact
SPOF	Single Point of Failure
TCU	Total Cost of Utilization
TSO	The Stationary Office
UC	Underpinning Contract
VBF	Vital Business Function
VCD	Variable Cost Dynamics

References

Bon, J. van, (Ed.) (2007). *Foundations of IT Service Management, Based on ITIL V3*. Zaltbommel: Van Haren Publishing for itSMF.

ITIL. Continual Service Improvement (2007). OGC. London: TSO.

ITIL. Service Design (2007). OGC. London: TSO.

ITIL. Service Operation (2007). OGC. London: TSO.

ITIL. Service Strategy (2007). OGC. London: TSO.

ITIL. Service Transition (2007). OGC. London: TSO.